The Fictional Writer's Primer

AND
How To Become
A Rich And Famous Author
Without Ever Really
Writing A Book

By Darvin P. Harfield and Adam Poszar

First Edition

Rabid Rhino Publishing, Huntington, Indiana

The Fictional Writer's Primer
And How To Become A Rich And Famous Author
Without Ever Really Writing A Book

By Darvin P. Harfield and Adam Poszar

Published by:

Rabid Rhino Publishing
Post Office Box 5013
Huntington, Indiana 46750-5013 U.S.A.

Publisher's Cataloging in Publication
(Prepared by Quality Books, Inc.)

Harfield, Darvin P.
   The fictional writer's primer ; and, How to become a rich and famous author without ever really writing a book / by Darvin P. Harfield and Adam Poszar. -- 1st ed.
   p. cm.
   Includes bibliographical references and index.
   Preassigned LCCN: 93-84934.
   ISBN 0-9637124-0-3

   1. Authorship--Handbooks, manuals, etc. 2. Authorship--Humor. I. Poszar, Adam. II. Title. III. Title: How to become a rich and famous author without ever really writing a book.

PN147.H37 1993   808.02'00207
                                          QBI93-1016

What others are saying about this book:

Best stuff we ever done!
American Jury Of Kindred Editors

The whole family loved yer book. 'Specially
after the Sears catalog got used up.
D. Authaus, Moosejaw, ND

Your book is great! My coffee table hardly
wobbles at all any more!
Erma Yankovitzch, Reading, PA

The Fictional Writer's Primer is the nicest gift
a mother could hope for, but 4,000 copies?
Mrs. Adam Poszar Sr., Tumbleweed City, TX

The Fictional what?
Chicago Some Times

We'd like to meet you, gentlemen, and soon!
Mr. Sam Hunter, Internal Revenue Service

"Tain't bad, fer bathroom readin'."
The Des Moines Hog Auction News

Contents

* Please see brief statement, bottom of Page 136.

ABOUT THE AUTHORS

Darvin P. Harfield is an attorney, husband, father of two, Board Chairman of the local bank, member of the Chamber of Commerce, Bar Association, Masons, Elks, Moose, Lions, VFW, PTA, ASPCA, Save the Wales Foundation, lives in a big white house with a picket fence, owns a red sub-compact car, writes an astronomy- turned-local-humor column for the area newspaper, reads a bunch, and is locally famous for all this. He has been unofficially credited with coining the phrases, *"Have a nice Autumnal Equinox"*, *"How may I be of applicability to you,"* *"I'll imbibe to that,"* and *"Sue the whelp of a canine's buns off"*. Mr. Harfield is also vastly disinterested in UFO's and extraterrestrial life.

Adam Poszar insists that he is not a retired used auto parts salesman, ex-Marine, nor self-educated brain surgeon. He has, however, been personally involved in the study of languages since the age of three, when he first threw a dish of alphabet soup from his feeding tray. His first nonfiction work (which he denies having written), The Frontal Lobotomy - An Owner's Guide, has been unanimously acclaimed among the experts as the definitive work addressing do-it-yourself brain surgery. The sequel, Done It, Now Where I am? will hit the book stands this fall.

He also insists that he really was born on Earth and that the large, glowing metallic object that hums in his garage is merely a planter designed to stimulate his Redwood seedlings. Mr. Poszar is not the least bit famous.

ACKNOWLEDGEMENTS

This book was produced with the assistance of the

American Jury Of Kindred Editors

in cooperation with the

Literary Intelligence Enhancement Society.

We wish also to publicly thank the many mentors, friends, relatives, customers, and business associates who have so greatly and magnanimously aided our writing careers that this book has finally been brought to fruition.

However, after having read the manuscript, they all asked that their names not be printed.

Actually they insisted.

Besides, nobody ever reads this page anyway.

DEDICATION

This book is dedicated to you who have written or are about to expend the effort involved in writing truly marvelous works but are slightly misinformed as to how to go about it and, once you do, how to get your work profitably published.

To you writers in search of illumination along your path to book authorship:

Welcome, our light is burning brightly.

We are, however, a little uncertain that anyone is home.

PREFACE

Why The Fictional Writer's Primer?

Adam's reply was, "Why not?"
Darv decided to put his reasons on paper. He is still
writing. The last time someone checked, he was on page 1,092.

This book began unintentionally as friendly letters
between two writers describing their experiences, observations,
opinions, and yes, frustrations as they struggled to become
published. What they learned about the writing and publishing
"industry" is that it's not all peaches and cream. It's more like
cooked spinach that's been sitting in the refrigerator for a couple
of weeks.

Their efforts have led them to the belief that above all,
writing must be fun, with a touch of craziness thrown in for spice.

Knowing that there are other writers also striving to
become authors, they feel that it is time they, too, had something
to help them laugh at the kinds of things that would be thought of
as insanity were they happening in any other industry, except
maybe the Federal government.

Our publisher has suggested that we describe this book
as a 'tongue-in-cheek' parody of the writing and publishing
industry intended to only poke fun at it in a 'Don't try any of this
at home' manner.

We refused.

Our tongues are sticking straight out.

INTRODUCTION

So, you want to be a rich and famous author.

Maybe you just want to free yourself from your pain-in-the-bucket, boring, forty-hour-a-week job. Maybe you're currently unemployed and don't really care to go through that old resume, appointment, interview, fill-out-this-form, sign-on-the-dotted-line ritual again.

You've either heard or read about all those authors who have struggled with two or more jobs, living in abject poverty, writing at the kitchen table for ten years or more, striving to get their first work published.

And you have probably been led to believe that this is what is required to 'make it'. In other words to amass fabulous fortunes, go on television talk shows, live in impressive homes, wear designer clothes, have tee shirts with your picture on them, drive expensive cars, and 'work' as long as three or four hours a day. And you've thought, "That's the life for me."

Well you can forget it.

Through the careful following of the instructions in this book you can do and have and buy all that stuff with much less work than that!

You see, some people actually write books, and take anywhere from eight months to twenty years or more doing it.

Why?

When, in this remarkable age of computerization, electronic high-speed mass communications, television, and mega-corporations one has the potential to become a famous author without ever actually writing a book! And we double your value!

You are actually holding two books bound into one!

In **Book One**, we describe how 'real' writers ply their trade AND we offer our unique Beat The System suggestions wherever possible.

Book Two will tell you the secrets, the things that have been tried by many, of becoming famous (and maybe rich) as an author without ever really actually writing a book.

Read on and we will show you how, with very little effort or creativity on your part, you too can achieve your dreams as an author without all the work, hassle, and headaches.

WARNING-DISCLAIMER

(Cop-Outs)

The purpose of this book is to entertain. Any instructions, hints, or recommendations herein are for entertainment purposes only.

Any resemblance to persons living or dead, including the authors, is purely coincidental.

None of the people involved in the writing, production,or distribution of this book may be held responsible in any way for anything that may or may not happen to the reader resulting from actually commiting any of the acts described in this book. In other words, if you really do any of the stuff described in this book, you do it at your own risk.

Information that may have any resemblance to actual fact is completely accidental.

We apologize for this bit of seriousness. We'll try not to let it happen again.

1

TITLES

In choosing an appropriate title for his/her work, an authentic author has to consider a word or phrase that will adhere to certain criteria.

Before we get into it, however, we offer you a challenge. If you are going to be so cotton-picking fussy that you sit still through this entire chapter to become so darned good at creating superlative titles that you get fan mail from real authors, first try putting your brain into high gear with an even more worthwhile project. Find a single, simple, easily pronounced, non-sexist word to replace "his/her" and "he/she".

According to our highly accurate research, the slash "/" key is the first to wear out on most keyboards. And, while we applaud efforts to be non-biased, gender-ly speaking, we crave a new word for the task. The last known similar effort resulted in the creation of "mizz" as in Ms. Jones. Again, we do not take issue with the idea, only its result. Not only does "mizz" dredge up all kinds of racist images, verbalizing it makes the authors sneeze. Now, back to the list of criteria for choosing a title for your work.

1. It must accurately describe or hint at the book's content, genre, story line, main character, and/or setting.

Or not. Consider such treasures as 'Dick and Jane', 'The Innocents Abroad', 'The Spy Who Came In From The Cold', and 'Plane Geometry—4th Edition'. These writers followed our rules and achieved great success.

Now look at 'Les Miserables' by some guy named Hugo. Ugh! We predict that this book will go nowhere. He wasn't careful enough to even spell the darned title right. It's so far out in left field that you'd think it was written in a foreign language! Follow the rules and the reader's interest will be captured. Better yet, the bookstore browser's attention will be grabbed.

2. Keep it short, four words maximum. Okay five, then, but no more. And absolutely no pre-Victorian style subtitles that rattle on and on and on making no further headway toward understanding, adding nothing more for the enjoyment of the reader, saying nothing new, just repeat-ing and repeating and repeating the same old thing, over, and over, and over, and over and over andoverandoverand over. . .

3. The title should be easy to pronounce. Unless you are an already published and very successful attorney, in which case you don't give a fat rat's fanny if anyone can understand what you say, much less pronounce your titles.

4. Finally, the title must be made to fit on the book's cover when blown up to a size that it can be read by myopics from a distance of two and a half city blocks. Remember that room must be left for the obligatory pictures of scantily clad women, giant fish, airplanes, drooling dogs, or AK47's.

TITLES CONTINUED

Wherein the Authors Elucidate
All Manner
of Other Considerations
in
The Selection of Titles

or

MORE ON TITLES

Which Selection Is Intended
by The Authors
To Convince The Reader
of
The Correctness of The Authors'
Formerly Stated Position
Regarding
Endless Pre-Victorian Style Titles

Some authors sincerely believe that one should not write even one page until the title has been chosen. Others write their entire books, deciding on a title only after the last period falls. Most, however, choose a title somewhere in between. Whether you choose to follow the dull, tired, boring path trod by 'real' writers or use our easy, fun, beat-the-system suggestions, you should have something legible prominently positioned atop your text by the time your manuscript is sent to the publisher, agent or whomever.

Picture your publisher hollering at his assistant, "Hey you! Hand me that Van Stuyvengardenburgher manuscript."

Instead, he can say, "Hey you! Hand me 'Catcher in the

Eye'. My kid can't reach the urinal in the men's room."

So now you are wondering, "When is the best time to pick a title?" Our brief but exhaustive study of all title development methods currently in use proves that it doesn't make a beaver's dam when you pick it.

HOW TO BEAT THE SYSTEM

If you decide to pick your title before writing your book, use our "Name the Rock Group" method. Pick up a dictionary and choose any two words at random. If you don't have a dictionary, use any other book. If you don't have any books, use the first two words that come to mind.

Write them down, separately and together in as many combinations as you can. (Of course there are only two combinations. We just wanted to see if you were paying attention.)

The next step is to juggle the syllables around in your mind and see what falls out. As an example, we did this with our dictionary and here's what happened. Randomly *(no kidding!)* the words chassis and mastitis were picked. We tossed them around and here are the results. Each title is followed by the story idea it created.

Cha Sis
A light hearted story told by the Mexican half-brother of a female Chinese dance instructor.

Cha Cha See
A little blind girl dances her way into the hearts of America and earns enough to pay for her sight-restoring eye surgery.

C.H. Assis
A ruthless industrialist strives to quench his lust for power through the unscrupulous buying and selling of companies to forge an all-powerful corporation.

Mast of the Titis

Underwater adventurers discover the remains of an ancient sailing vessel and learn its mysteries, all the while thanking God for the invention of fiberglass.

Mass for the Tightest

A disgruntled priest delivers a blockbuster sermon that shakes loose the purses of his penny-pinching parishioners to save a nearby convent. Spencer Tracy would have taken the lead in the movie version.

Cha See Ma's Titties

Biography of a Hong Kong stripper.

Ma's Tightest Chassis

The history of the invention of undergarments for full-figured women, subtitled 'Whalebone to Spandex'.

As you can see, a surprising variety of subjects can come from a mere two words.

But what if you already have an idea for a book? Or maybe you've even gone so far as actually writing something, which seems a tad foolish to us. All you need to do is follow the above suggestions backward! It's easy. Pick maybe six or eight words out of what you have written and combine them in pairs until one of the pairs looks right. Here's an example.

I have an idea for a story about Jo. Jo is a bionic bear. Jo travels from planet to planet and from star system to star system, whatever the hell a star system is. She attempts to mate with the creatures she meets. This is not only because she is extremely lonely. She is also intent on creating the first biological/bionic master race of bear/whatevers.

Here are a few of the sure-to-sell titles we developed from just this brief description.

Star Mates	**Sex In HyperSpace**
Bionic Love	**Pregnant on Xerkgup**
The Sex	**The Boys From**
Machine	**Brapdyl**

See how easy that is!

Things to Avoid:

As with most anything you do, there are things that you should try to avoid when picking your titles. Here is an exhaustive list:

Any and all swear-words, cursing, or expletives.
All words that start with the letter 'Q.'
All words ending with the letter 'Q'.
Any word having more than four syllables.
The same title as anything that is currently or ever has been published.
Any and all words having anything to do, no matter how remotely, with sleep, relaxation, snoring, non-sexual human horizontalness, or teachers' salaries.

One Final Thought:

Whether you choose your title by following the old boring method or use our quick, easy, fun way, there is one last little detail that you should remember.

YOUR PUBLISHER WILL CHANGE IT ANYWAY!

2

GENRE

So, you've decided to be a writer.

Your mother has already laughed in your face at the notion. Your father is fretting over the money he spent to educate you for a real job. Your spouse has given you the obligatory encouragement, secretly hoping that this latest obsession will not be as expensive as the others. And you have already practiced autographing book jackets.

If you're male, you have hidden in your closet a pair of dusty Oxford loafers, a bottle of cheap scotch, a pair of wide-wale corduroy slacks, a camel sportcoat (with leather elbow patches), a silk shirt, and a pipe. Everything you will need to go on the TV talk show circuit.

If you are female, the far corner of your closet boasts a mid-calf black skirt, tall boots, a faded maroon paisley blouse, and a flaming red scarf. And you have begun using your maiden name again.

You have even considered quitting your job, to allow you more time for cashing that first big advance check, once you've found a publisher.

You have a pile of typing paper handy, your dictionary is standing ready beside the keyboard. Your thesaurus is gone, either thrown out with the pile of old sale catalogs or serving as the replacement for the leg that broke off the TV last month. You are truly ready.

Hold on just a minute there, Buckaroo! There are a few things yet to be done.

"Such as?" you may ask.

Such as deciding what to write, Buford. We offer the following general guide to assist you in making your decision.

1. Plain Old Novel.

Advantages: No accuracy required. Just make it up. Copy that little slogan from the front of some other book. You know, the one that talks about any resemblance to any actual event or person, dead or alive, being purely coincidental. This will place your book solidly into the "pack of lies" category.

Disadvantages: Requires imagination and skill. Novels are also too darned long.

2. Historical Novel.

Advantages: You will be considered very smart by friends and relatives, even if it's never published. Cover designs are fun to choose if you like battle scenes.

Disadvantages: Research is normally required. Dialogue may require extra effort to be historically accurate. One should not, for example, have Cecil Rhodes say, "What a rad little country! Let's screw it up."

3. Romance Novel.

Advantages: Sexually fulfilling. Cover designs are easy to choose as all are basically the same.

Disadvantages: The money will spoil you. Your mother will lie about your job. "My son is a veterinarian," her neighbor says. "What does your daughter do, Inez?" "Uh, she's a, ah, you know, a — stockbroker, that's what she is, a stockbroker."

4. Non-fiction or "Real" books.
Advantages: None.
Disadvantages: Non-fiction doesn't sell as well as novels.
And you normally have to know what you're writing about to do one.

5. Short Stories.
Advantages: They're short.
Disadvantages: So how many of these things can Reader's
Digest and New Yorker magazines print in a month anyway?

6. Magazine or Newspaper Articles.
Advantages: The gratification of seeing your name widely
printed.
Disadvantages: Pays less than minimum wage. Letters to
the editor criticizing your work embarrass your family. Publishers
take an average of 83 years to respond to your submission query.

7. Cookbook or How-To.
Advantages: Easy.
Disadvantages: None.

Since this book deals primarily with fiction (had you noticed?), we will stick with that topic. Unless of course, we decide not
to. Accordingly, we offer the following considerations which form
the heart of this book, along with all the other chapters, the index,
table of contents, foreword, prefaces, appendix, introductions, and
all the other stuff.

This book has a big heart, but no liver. The pancreas may
also be found to be lacking. For additional information, see the
Appendix on page 137.

One of the first concerns an author has to deal with is
choosing a genre. Genre is pronounced *jon-rah*. To those of you with
small children at home, it initially brings to mind your reaction to the
little one's first successful use of the potty chair - the toilet cheer.

Setting any similarities aside, there are numerous genre in the book industry. Certain kinds of stories are read by certain subcultures or segments of society. Genre are used to approximately describe that which is written for and read by the various subcultures out there in Bookstore Land. New ones pop up and old ones die out regularly. And they overlap. Frankly speaking, they change so fast that nobody can keep accurate track of them.

Various genre have, however, become solidified to the extent that in order to write for them, the author must adhere to imposed regulations covering general plot, character do's and don'ts, number of pages, size of chapters, etc. If, of course, he/she wants to have his/her work published. Breaking the mold is for the independently wealthy willing to write until their money runs out.

Here is a rough list of the current major genre and a brief description of the subcultures that read them. The material for this section is based on painstaking research that should be footnoted. However, neither of the authors can remember how to do footnotes properly, so that topic will not be covered herein.

Gothic Romance

These are love stories set in the British Isles and sold in American supermarket aisles. Everything that happens happens in either the Eighteenth or Nineteenth Century. A young woman travels to a castle via sailing ship, is threatened by a dashing hunk, is swept into additional adventures, has a change of heart regarding the hunk, is saved by same, falls in love and happily ever-afters. This is a very structured genre. Books written for it must be exactly so many pages long. The young woman enters the castle no later than chapter two and is threatened in chapter three. The additional adventures must occur between chapters four and six. She may be a non-virgin only if widowed before the book begins. Her change of heart and rescue may happen anywhere in chapters seven through ten. Falling in love, chapters eleven and twelve. Happily ever-aftering occurs in chapter thirteen. And although it may be delicately hinted at, deflowering is never described. Gothic romances are read by women between the ages of twenty-one and forty-five, and those who get their second wind after sixty. They are also read by men who play Barry Manilow records in the background.

Historic Romance

This genre is identical to Gothic Romance with the single exception being the setting, which can be anywhere on this planet. Although explicit sex is forbidden, every word not involved in historical description must be designed to make hormones flow like the River Styx in flood. In other words, soap operas with a lesson.

Western

This genre is set in America in the mid-1800's. It includes cowboys, Indians, horses, saloons, and guns. It also includes young range widows that no man would touch due to of respect for womanhood and all it stands for, and dance-hall girls who every man touches due to testosterone poisoning caused by the young range widows. Books must include long travel over snow-capped mountains (preferably on foot) and scorching deserts (carrying an empty canteen), at least three gunfights, two love scenes (one failed, one successful), and two fistfights. It must involve a hero who is tough as last week's pizza crust, but with a heart as tender as a new blade of grass. Westerns are read primarily by men who possess either a fetish for guns, a love of violence, a need for simplicity, the conviction that they were born a hundred years too late, or any combination of these. If historical romances can be termed "lady" books, Westerns are "Macho-Man". And don't yew fergit it pard!

Science Fiction

This genre has grown and evolved tremendously within the past few years. This has been attributed to the Xgokynug Snekfluwq factor, the driving force behind SciFi popularity. Virtually no one in the industry can pronounce, much less define it. The only presently applicable restrictions are that books must make only passing mention of life on earth and should include a robot in some way, shape, or form. The robot should, however, appear to be something else, such as an aspirin bottle. These books are read mainly by men who possess either a fetish for rayguns, the love of violence, a need for complexity, or the conviction that they were born a hundred years too early.

Action/Adventure

These books are centered around men at war. Extreme violence and carnage are the norm. The hero is always someone who looks like a bodybuilding champion but didn't have to do all the work. Weapons and their creative uses abound, severed limbs and other body parts are as common as cuss words. The setting is immaterial as it will be leveled by the final chapter anyway.

The cultural subgroup of readers consists mostly of men who:

1. Work in an office.
2. Wear glasses, usually thick ones.
3. Weigh less than a hundred and twenty pounds or more than three hundred.
4. Possess large adams apples or double chins that bob up and down as they read.
5. Claim that they used to play football, but were actually equipment managers for the J.V. team.
6. Are proud that they can read in spite of never going beyond the 9th grade.

Fantasy

Almost anything goes here, from dragons, sorcerers, and living gargoyles to the spirits of long dead Egyptian ancestors with psychokinetic powers. Setting is normally Europe in the Dark Ages. A lot of these books sell, but nobody other than people who have been institutionalized for chronic mental disturbances and college freshmen will admit to reading them.

Scare Your Pants Off

This genre has also grown quite rapidly in the recent past. Take anything that is basically innocent and/or harmless. Have it kill a lot of people with as much gore as possible. High school cheerleaders and other alleged virgins are the preferred victims. Have the hero or heroin find its secret, chase it, suffer because of it, wrestle with it, and destroy it forever. On the last page hint that it wasn't really destroyed. Sequels sell. Readers of this kind of novel are the same as those of Romance novels except that they are bored with reading about castles full of thirty year old virgins and well-mannered ghosts.

Tear Your Pants Off

These books are always written with taste. In this genre taste is normally described as either sweet/sour or salty. Its subgroup of readers is divided into three groups. Men under the age of sixteen, men over the age of sixteen, and women who find where the men have hidden them.

Mystery

Another solid yet growing genre, mysteries include the following. Somebody gets killed. The person who has done it is either caught or also dies. The challenge in writing for this genre is in devising increasingly creative substances, weapons, or situations wherein murder can occur and in seeing how little connective tissue, and how much wild coincidence, can be used as evidence in the discovery and possible capture of the perpetrator. A reminder for anyone who wants to write for this genre. The butler never does it. Readership includes people possessing either an infatuation with the creative bringing-about of death or those who find themselves stuck in an unhappy relationship.

Spy Stories

Assume that other novels can be diagramed as beautiful roads with graceful, sweeping curves; with exits and entrances that blend subplots in and out of the main storyline and clover-leaves and overpasses to smooth the traffic. Spy stories can then be diagramed as roads wandering aimlessly only to simultaneously converge into one unmarked intersection —BAMM! They are usually cluttered with wrecked sports cars and battered pedestrians. People who buy these books play chess when they aren't reading.

Sports Stories.

These books are targeted for the class of Americans with the most disposable income, adolescent boys. They always have two authors. For example, 'How I Became Da Welterweight Champeen Of Da Whole World An' Udder Stuff' by Spike "Hammerhands" McGurk as told to Simon St. Christopher. Cover illustration by Mercy Hospital Plastic Surgery Ward.

Mainstream or General Fiction

This classification covers books that just don't fit into any of those mentioned above for a variety of reasons. The castle is located Missouri, the cowboy doesn't carry a gun, the virgin turns out to be a hooker, the rabid dog dies in chapter three instead of fifteen, or whatever. Unfortunately, no one either in or out of the book industry can come up with an accurate description of the subculture attached to it. This genre does have its merits, however. Read on.

Non-Fiction

Needless to say, this term covers a lot of ground. It includes topics such as travel, science, history, needlepoint, dog training, and autobiographies of people who have been taken aboard intergalactic soup cans and molested by eight-legged aardvarks that speak Portuguese. It does not include, and should never be confused with, books about astrology, new-age anything, economics, psychology, or politics. True non-fiction books are purchased only by college professors, who hollow them out and use them as hiding places for the stuff they collect while on sabbatical.

BEATING THE SYSTEM

Mix things up. Its easy. Its fun. And it will increase the number of people who will read your masterwork.

Have the ghost of a cowboy possess the body of a two hundred pound flea posing as an English butler stranded on another planet.

Create a beautiful twenty-five year old virgin, preferably from the deep South, and have her ride down the Mississippi alone in a Viking warship to do battle against a one-armed Captain in the Confederate Army with whom she finds an inexplicable sexual attraction and in whom she finds her long lost brother.

The music from a child's windup toy sends off the exact vibrations to trigger the sonic release on Russia's nuclear missiles creating total destruction of the World's major cities. Have the sole survivors, the child, an international double agent, and a lonely young range widow begin a new world order based on a love of rap music.

See? Easy, simple, and fun! Every market is captured. Feel free to use any of these ideas for yourself, we ask only that you give us 10% of your gross earnings. Darv can be reached at his regular job, Adam at his trailer.

3
WHERE TO WRITE

EDITOR'S NOTE:

There is a difference of opinion between authors. And neither will budge. Hence, the opinions of each will follow separately. I apologize if this causes any confusion. I cannot afford to replace my office furniture.

Darv:

Once, in a desperate bid to lose weight, one of the authors bought a cassette series that was guaranteed to make him a thin person. In the first cassette, he was instructed in the fine art of self-hypnosis. It proved to be the core of this particular method of diet. After the relaxation process, his first instruction was to imagine a place, in great detail, where he could go to sort out his thoughts. He constructed a glass-wrapped room on top of a tower overlooking an endless tidal marsh on one side, and a bank of purple foothills rising to the horizon on the other. He didn't lose a lot of weight, but he did learn to create a perfect environment for writing, even if it was constructed of ether.

In practice, of course, a writer can't often write in places of such serene beauty. More often he sits at his desk (or the kitchen table) with telephones buzzing, doors slamming, children screaming, too hot, too cold, the sun in his eyes, or with the view of a spreading stain on the ceiling caused by a leaky roof.

The writer should have a special place to write. It should be one that is used for no other purpose. Pay your bills at the desk, but write your book on the card table. All of the materials you will need should be at your fingertips; reference books, paper, keyboard, telephone, M&M's, and a very large wastebasket.

If you cannot afford to have such a place then have a special time when the space is yours and yours alone, and free of interruptions. Some people write in their heads, translating the product to physical record later on. Others write as they think. (Yes, and some write without thinking.)

Either way, getting words on paper -or computer disk- requires seclusion. As the pressures of family may not allow one to write at home, the best production may come while at the office. If one is fortunate enough to be self-employed, simply bark out "No calls!", close the door, and enjoy your solitude. Or do as Adam does—write at work during lunch break.

(Adam's first interjection)
This is a good idea even though it no longer applies. See my second interjection.

Darv
Best of all, if your employer maintains two places of business, do this. Tell the boss at location A that you are spending the day at location B. Tell the boss at location B you are spending the day at location A. Stay home and write while the rest of your family is off at school or work. This constitutes stealing from your employer of course, but a decent writer is capable of rationalizing any behavior. After all, each of us loves Huck Finn, and he was a pipe smoking truant.

(Adam's second interjection)
Now do you see why the earlier idea no longer applies?

Darv

The writer must guard against using the lack of a suitable workplace as an excuse not to write. "I'll pack up my tweed jacket with the leather elbow patches, my bottle of vintage scotch, my English Setter, and my old Underwood and spend my vacation alone in a cabin in the woods just writing and writing", the writer tells himself.

In reality he spends it marveling enviously at the college students sweeping up cigarette butts with those nifty long-handled dust pans at a large theme park while his kids whine with fatigue and beg for money. It is just as well. If he were ever to really spend his week or two in a cabin, he would end up swatting mosquitoes, rearranging the cabin after a visit from raccoons, or leaving early because a family of skunks have made their home just under the floorboards.

The perfect workplace is not, after all, a place. It is an attitude. Many an author can create a heroine who is beautiful and irresistibly seductive after spending eight days in the jungle escaping from cannibals, miles from the nearest toothbrush, razor, or antiperspirant deodorant stick. Therefore you are certainly capable of creating the perfect writing environment, wherever you may be.

Adam

Thank you Mr. Harfield for telling the world about my recent career change, I really appreciate it. By the way, tomato juice really does remove skunk smell. Leaves your underwear a funny color, though.

Where to write is the second most important decision you will make concerning your efforts, right behind how much to charge for your written masterpieces. It must be a special place where your creative juices can flow unabated without hindrance or interruption. It will affect not only the flow but the slant and content of your work. I repeat, your choice is critical!

The best way to locate your perfect writing space is through use of the scientific method. That's right, trial and error. Pick a place,

35

any place. How about the great outdoors?

Grab a tablet and pencil and drive to the nearest state or county park. Walk to the local cemetery. Set yourself down on the steps of the county courthouse. Parks are great places to write if you don't mind all the racket those damned squirrels, rabbits, chipmunks and birds make. Cemeteries tend to be a little quieter.

The county courthouse steps are the best. Not only is there an abundance of fresh air, people walking by will stop and ask you what the hell you think you are doing. This is a great way to build your reputation as a writer to be reckoned with.

Want to go out but remain indoors? My favorite places are the local library, bus stop, or train depot. The library is quiet, but they eventually close. I'm telling you this because, if you have chosen a seat that happens to be in a secluded corner, and especially if you should just happen to doze off, nobody will tell you. You will then be faced with the decision to stay and having to explain where you were to your spouse (You spent the night WHERE? Oh *SURE!*) or to escape, thereby setting off all the alarms for a five-mile radius. In which case the police are sure to be sitting just outside the door, you are arrested, and spend the next day explaining to your spouse (You spent the night *WHERE?*).

Should the bus stop or train depot be more to your liking (most are open 24 hours), remember to leave all your valuables at home.

In desperation, some writers have been known to rent a room in a hotel or motel in which to write. This should allow you enough quiet and solitude to complete at least a hundred pages. If for some odd reason you don't have a minimum of one hundred pages to show for your efforts, throw away the motel receipt and tell your spouse that you were arrested for breaking out of the library.

Maybe you would rather write at home. If you do, NEVER write at the kitchen table. A manuscript that looks as if it has been dipped in your favorite condiment will not be read favorably by an editor. The only exception is if you are writing an in depth review of the fast food industry, or if your favorite condiment is dijon mustard, which is currently in vogue with editors.

If you insist on seclusion, why not try the attic? NOBODY goes there. And, if your attic is anything like mine, all you need to do to jar that recalcitrant idea loose is merely stand up. The key to finding a place to write is be flexible and open minded.

(Darv's first interjection)
Did I not just say that same thing?

Adam
Once I even tried writing in the basement. There was a terrible storm going on at the time which made the rest of the house unsuitable, due to the noise. The basement was quiet, even if it was a bit damp. I recall being relaxed yet alert as I typed my story, stretched out on an old air mattress I found, floating around the furnace. It was a bit hard on the electric typewriter, though.

This experiment actually led to the discovery of the finest place of all in which to write. It seem as though I accidentally let one foot dangle off the edge of the air mattress a bit too long and something bit me. I got a considerable amount of writing done throughout the following weeks in the hospital, when I was conscious. Hospitals are by far the best places in which to write. They are quiet, you rarely hit your head, people are friendly, nobody will arrest you or steal your clothes, and nothing will bite you.

It is not recommended, however, due to the inherent difficulty of admission without an up-to-date insurance card printed in triplicate, which covers every ailment known to doctordom and nursehood.

How about writing right in the center of the living or family room? Creating the next Great American Novel is the perfect excuse to stifle the kids, get your spouse to wait on you hand and foot, or shoo them all to their rooms, in which case you get to watch what you want on the television.

The best way is to try a variety of times and places. If you do and still can't find a suitable time and place in which to write, don't worry. Don't write. Book Two of this volume will tell you how you can become a rich and famous author without all that work.

By the way, wherever you choose to write, a loud statement to the effect of, "My whole career and all of your futures are riding on this!" is a great way to get those within earshot to bend to your will.

A final note:
If you try Darvin's diet plan, don't make your special place a restaurant.

(Darv's final interjection)
I (chomp chomp chomp) agree!

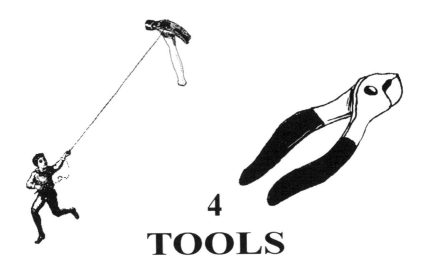

4
TOOLS

Tools are available to the writer, some essential, some optional, some mere luxuries. There are so many, in fact, we have chosen to organize our treatment of writing tools based on cost, usability, and value.

The first question one must ask before starting a career in writing is, "How do I know what I will have to spend?" We have designed a way for you to calculate it almost to the penny.

First, total your monthly income.

Second, subtract your essential monthly bills, such as mortgage, car, groceries, and utilities.

Third, subtract your miscellaneous expenses such as clothing, medical, entertainment, psychiatric therapy, electrolysis, and so forth.

Fourth, label the remaining amount as your Monthly Writing Career Allowance. Assuming you are truly dedicated to becoming a bona fide writer, you can double it, for expense planning purposes.

Fifth and finally, multiply it by twelve to get your Yearly Writing Career Fund.

To determine the amount you will actually spend, take your Yearly Writing Career Fund and square it.

Yes dear reader, accurate almost to the penny.

We have outlined four groups of tools according to affordability. Each group will get you started.

Package A
Super Saver Economy Writer's Starter Kit

98 grocery bags	Cost: free, if you know where to look.
1 box crayons	Cost: $ 1.59.
Total expense	$ 1.59.

Notes: There is one major hidden expense here. Most publishers will refuse to read a manuscript that is not typed. Hiring a qualified typist can cost anywhere from fifty cents to five dollars per typed page. We recommend that you locate a friend or relative who can actually type and bet them a 'stake' dinner that they can't type your novel in two days or less. If they should somehow happen to win the bet, sharpen one end of a wooden stick and send it to them with one of those little packets of your favorite condiment. (These, with the exception of dijon mustard, can be economically obtained from your favorite fast-food restaurant.) A word of caution: since you will possibly use more than just the black crayon, we strongly recommend that you choose a typist who is not colorblind.

If you want to go hog wild you can embellish the list of materials by purchasing a 99 cent pair of scissors. This way you can cut the bags into pages and add a more professional look to your work, which will impress your typist.

Package B
Economy Beginning Writer's Kit

One used typewriter, manual, with ribbon.
One package typing paper, clean both sides.
One eraser, large.
One dictionary, abridged.
One How To Write a Book book (ours).
Two bottles of wine.
Total expense $ 25.00 to $ 50.00, depending on your choice of wine.

Notes: Thanks to the onslaught of electronic word processors, used typewriters can be obtained almost for free. The best places we have found are fishing boat rental businesses. You will often find typewriters tied to long ropes, at the back of the boats just below the old cottage cheese containers where last month's worms are forming little paisley marks on the waxed cardboard. Many a shrewd author has negotiated a successful trade using things as inexpensive as a concrete block.

Typing paper prices have recently dropped for the same reason as typewriter costs.

If you don't want to spend the 50 cents for a good eraser either make up your mind at the start that you are under no circumstances going to make a mistake or snip one off the end of the pencil at the bank. These are easy to find, as banks always chain them to the counter tops.

The dictionary, we admit, is optional. Remember, however, that even a cheap one will look spiffy on your bookshelf.

The How To Write a Book book (this one) is, as you have by now seen, invaluable and well worth its trifling price. Besides, you've already bought it.

The wine is, of course, strictly for medicinal purposes.

The only hidden expense in this list has to do with the age of the typewriter ribbon. Herein lies proof of our great forethought in recommending a manual typewriter. Hit the keys harder and don't worry about it. With a little practice and a small, inexpensive piece of charcoal, you can easily make the pages legible. Or, if you have bought port wine, you can soak the ribbon in the bottle overnight. If you are desperate (no charcoal, prefer white wine) soak your ribbon in lemon juice and warm the pages over a candle.

Package C
Intermediate Writer's Kit

One new electric typewriter with self-correcting feature and built-in dictionary.
Ten packages typing paper.
One dictionary, unabridged.
One thesaurus, not to be opened until your death.
One punctuation manual, or an employable 5th grade student.
Three How-To-Write-a-Book books, one of which is ours.
One newspaper annual subscription.
One coffee maker.
Twenty pounds coffee.
One table or desk, big and gnarly, with cigarette burns.
One chair.
Four bottles of wine.
Total expense $ 716.00 to $ 2135.00

Notes: We admit, the self-correcting electric typewriter is easier and faster, and it will save you the expense of buying, or the trouble of stealing, erasers.

Open nine of your ten packages of typing paper. Fill one page with words in any order and place it face up on top. That way anybody who might look in on you will see that you have been hard at work. Sacrificing a dozen pages to wad into balls and strew about the wastebasket also adds a professional touch, but be sure to rumple your hair to complete the effect.

The unabridged dictionary is to show you more of the words that you aren't spelling correctly. The dictionary in your word processor is used to correct typos. If you are lucky enough to have one handy, the 5th grader can do both.

The thesaurus is to throw off any competitors who may be spying on your workplace. It is also quite handy should you lose a leg from your big, gnarly desk.

The punctuation manual and the other two How-To-Write-a-Book books are strictly for show. The newspaper will give you something to do while you are searching for thoughts, contemplating your next twist of plot, fine-tuning your characters or twiddling your toes.

The coffee maker, especially if it is the kind that gurgles, will lead others to think that you are actually in there working on your novel. The twenty pounds of coffee (remember to add water and follow the manufacturers instructions) will help you stay awake nights as you attempt to figure how to pay for all this stuff. Nighttime is also the time to write, since you will be working at a paying job during the day.

The table or desk and chair will keep you from otherwise looking ridiculous by sitting on the floor.

The wine is for the celebration that will occur either when you've sold your first book or when you finally realize that you really can't pay for all this stuff.

Package D
Full Blown No-Holds-Barred
Experienced Writers Set

This is a concise listing of the basic necessities owned by those whose books are regularly published, or so they claim. This is according to our thorough and scientific studies, each of which began with the following two questions: "Hey, Adam? and "Hey, Darv?".

One MultiMegabitbyte Computer with: 808868 high speed microprocessor, 20 inch color monitor with at least one "G" in its acronymic name, 110 megabyte hard disk, 64,000 bit per second modem, XALT keyboard, Superfont 360 word per second letter quality laser printer.

One spare of the above.

Four different and incompatible word processor programs.

Five computer video game programs.

Seven boxes of computer paper with annoying perforated edges.

Three of each: Dictionary, unabridged, Thesaurus, Grammar text, Punctuation text.

112 leather bound used books, preferably written in French, Latin, or German.

Four major metropolitan newspaper subscriptions.

Twelve miscellaneous magazine subscriptions

One issue of 'New Yorker', always left on the top of the stack.

Two cases of business envelopes, engraved.

Two cases of 9 inch by 12 inch manuscript mailers.

A cousin in the Postal Department.

A brother-in-law in publishing.

Two cases of expensive imported wine.

Twenty-three to thirty-five How-to-Write-a-Book books.

A private office.

A wide screen television with built-in VCR.

An assortment of videotapes, none of which are rated "G", "PG", or "PG-13".

A library that consists of several hundred volumes including the following:

> The complete works of William Shakespeare, Dr. Spok, Thoreau, Tolstoy, Poe, Dickens, Homer, Toffler, and Shelley. It should also include Tolkien, Vonnegut, and Seuss. Ownership of these, however, is never admitted to.

A classy looking oak cabinet with a lock. This is where the 'National Enquirer', Ding-Dongs, and 'TV Guide' are hidden.

Total cost: Ranges from slightly more than the combined

national budgets of seven South American countries that don't export illegal drugs to slightly less than that of one that does.

Notes:

The usage description here is unavoidably brief.

The electronic word processor has undoubtedly torn down more physical barriers to writing than any other tool since the creation of the phonetic alphabet.

Notwithstanding, the vast complexity of computers can be a real pain to the average adult. As in our previous listing, the services of the typical 5th grader may prove invaluable.

5
CHARACTERS

Non-fiction writers might be tempted to pass over this chapter, feeling that it doesn't apply to them. (The little voice in the back of their minds probably saying, "Not my job, man.") But even in writing a newspaper article there is considerable latitude in the choice and development of their subjects; whom to interview, which opinion to stress, how much of both the subject's (and the writer's) personality to reveal, etc. Furthermore, if you actually bought this book you should try to get your money's worth out of it. That means read the whole thing.

If you have borrowed this book from a friend or the local library, do whatever you want, Cheapskate.

'Real' writers are supposedly capable of creating entire universes in print. Fuzzy little creatures resembling pug-nosed rats without tails that dress in royal garb and speak a never-before-heard, yet ancient language. Beautiful seductive women willing to do anything to get to the top of the social pecking order or land the man of their dreams. The universe saved at the very last possible moment by a dashing intergalactic garbage scow pilot and his abominable snowman sidekick. Depending on genre (and occasionally gender), the creation of believable characters is another tightly regulated, time consuming chore for 'genuine' writers.

EDITOR'S NOTE:

The authors, Adam and Darvin, disagree as to the best procedure for character creation. Each feels so strongly as to the superiority of his own method that my best efforts at reconciliation and compromise resulted in one breaking into tears and holding his breath until he passed out and the other smashing every piece of furniture in my office! I will not dignify these actions by telling who did what. For the sake of fairness and my new office, each will describe his preferred method.

Darvin

Once you determine the primary story line, or plot, you will have a firm idea as to whom the characters will be. In other words, the story will define the characters. For those who prefer to write a book without thinking, this technique will sound like work - and it is. But there are many side benefits to be gained from it. After all, if The Maker had not wanted us to think then why did He/She provide us with bathrooms in which to do so. Many How-To-Write-A-Book books suggest that after you complete your rough story outline your next step should be to prepare a detailed dossier on each character, no matter how minor. The dossier will give a physical description and a complete and detailed biography of the character. The idea is when you then complete your detailed story outline and start writing you will have a much better visual and historical picture of your characters in mind, and thus can do a better job developing each through the story. Also, introduction of a character in the beginning of your book or story as a red headed oil well rigger and later reference to the same character as a brunette lesbian dog walker is not considered great literature by most critics. The dossier will help keep them straight, if you remember to refer to it each time you return to a given character.

When a publisher tells you that he or she likes your work but that you need to make it longer, your initial reaction may be one of panic. And understandably so. You have spent two years of your otherwise normal life crafting a leak-proof plot.

Like the pioneers of yore, you have filled all the chinks between the logs, and no light shines through the roof. All the subplots come together in a nifty little steeple on top of the roof. It is done. Now some egghead from New York tells you to add fifty pages. Relax, it is only a temporary condition. The extra fifty pages are needed so the editor can cut them out and throw them away later. But it still has to fit. How do you expand your cabin without stretching the seams and making it leak?

ADD CHARACTERS!

It will give the story more life and greater depth. (The exact meaning of these phrases are universally unknown. Nonetheless they are repeated often and with feeling in most publisher-writer conversations.) Unfortunately, it also gives you another pile of those damned dossiers to create. An example is called for:

You first wrote: "Gladys walked the two blocks to her car, oblivious to the mist falling upon her uncovered head."

Instead you write: "As Gladys walked the two blocks to her car, oblivious to the mist falling upon her uncovered head, she became acutely aware of the bag lady shuffling along the sidewalk on the other side of the street. The crone stared at Gladys openly, rheumy eyes following her every step."

Now you can diverge, developing a micro-mini-sub-plot, or just painting a portrait of the old woman. Possibly contrasting her poverty with Gladys's affluence. Maybe it causes Gladys to fear for her future. You must be careful to do this artfully.

Think if it as adding a room to your cabin, rather than slapping up an outhouse on the side of the hill down the path.

Characters in your story range from the obvious principals to the most trivial and (without turning your work into a Russian novel with a nightmare of names) their addition is an effective way to accomplish certain ends.

"Brad took his seat in the First Class cabin of the airplane. He was wearing a black suit with a red carnation." Boring, boring.

"Brad took his seat in the First Class cabin of the airplane. The tiny elderly woman in the window seat moved her knitting bag to make room for him, thinking what a stark contrast the red carnation in his lapel made against his expensive black suit; not unlike the silk kerchief her long-dead husband had habitually carried in his breast pocket." Better, yes?

Development of major characters is of course a much larger task than some bit player tacked on later. Such considerations as philosophy of life, manner of speech, physical attributes and limitations, childhood background and occupational outlook become essential to the task (and therefore merit inclusion in your dossiers) of bringing to them the wholeness of existence attributed to fully functional personalities as the result of genuine life.

Due to a condition so slight that it doesn't deserve mention, I am trying like crazy to avoid the use of a certain overworked term. This is why the earlier sentence appears to carry on indefinitely. If you can stomach it, please feel free to substitute the phrase "of fleshing out the character" after the word `task'.

If you are writing non-fiction these considerations will be based on a real subject and must be accurate, or at the very least fairly derived from your observations. Otherwise the phrase "sue your buns off" will become quite familiar to you in the future.

In writing non-fiction, however, you do retain the author's prerogative in determining how much of the character's character to reveal, so creativity is still allowed to beat within your breast, however sickly.

An alternative to writing a dossier regarding a fictional character is to simply use a real person as your model. Here's how it works.

Firmly plant in your mind a picture of your recently widowed Aunt Bertha, complete with her extra chins, great rolls of flesh at the back of her hairy arms that billow from the sleeves of her tacky house dress, annoying laugh that sounds remarkably like an attack of whooping cough, and the indescribable smell of her kitchen. Beneath this mental picture, create a neon sign that blinks 'Danielle Dumdum', the main character of your story. Much easier than fiddling with a cumbersome dossier, and it will serve you well throughout the book as you can easily conjure up an accurate picture of Aunt Bertha at any time, without looking at a dossier.

The method does, however, have its drawbacks. Despite the vast effort and inconvenience it may require, you must prevent Aunt Bertha from reading your story, particularly if she happens to be filthy rich and you are named in her will. Remember the ancient proverb: Inheriting big bucks beats the tar out of working for a living.

It does not require mental gymnastics to take the next step of logic. If you pattern your characters after real people, pattern them after illiterate ones whenever possible. Also you must force yourself not to laugh out loud when you first open your new book and read the following words: "All characters are fictional. Any resemblance to real persons, living or dead, is purely coincidental."

Flaws are important, too. When developing a character, whether you choose the dossier, living model, or some other seat-of-the-pants method, the temptation is to create a character who is likable in every way. Much greater depth can be developed if even the hero of your story is given some minor flaws.

At this point I would like to make some distinctions regarding the use of flaws. If this should by some chance further confuse you, don't panic. You are free to look for additional explanation in our next book. Unfortunately, the next book we have planned has nothing whatever to do with the inclusion of physical and/or character flaws, or the art of writing for that matter. You are, however free to look.

Any character defects or physical abnormalities may safely be used if for descriptive purposes only. To wit: "The old man, his leathery skin dappled by dark age spots, shuffled down the path, gripping his cane with a claw-like hand and muttering curses at the small children playing in the park."

51

Defects used for specific purposes, such as to create hatred or endearment, to add definition to or ridicule a character must be chosen with delicacy to avoid alienating the reader or bringing pain to innocent people in the real world.

Above all else, never poke fun at those who are unfortunate enough to be, without any fault of their own and despite their greatest efforts, slightly overweight.

Also be certain to mentally distinguish flaws of character from flaws physical. Defective character traits typically define the bad guys but must be chosen with care if used to describe a good one. "Delilah told her mother she was going to the store, lying as usual," does not endear the character to the reader.

"Delilah told her mother she was going to the store, knowing her mother would suffer greatly if she knew the truth," makes Delilah more acceptable. Choosing physical defects must be done with care.

I once read a book wherein the protagonist was married to a woman who was beautiful and an excellent mother and wife, never complaining, always ready to support her husband in every endeavor. Boring, to say the least.

Apparently the author agreed, feeling that he must give this otherwise perfect person a flaw. He gave her a deformed, protruding shoulder blade that stuck out like a wing that her husband was forever caressing as they plodded through the book's plot. What a dumb devise.

Giving a good guy a physical flaw is fine, but such patronizing and ridiculous stuff as a fencing scar on one cheek, a pot belly, or wing-like shoulder blade detracts from the story, if not from the character.

A soft voice, fleeting memory, missing digit, or even blindness - these are "acceptable" handicaps if not overdone or ridiculed. An old device, common in the horror genre, is to give a terrible persona a terrible exterior such as an empty eye socket or a horribly scarred face. Hunchbacks, deaf mutes, and dwarfs peopled the books of the last century and the early decades of this.

But to use the same method to create feelings of hatred or disgust today is considered a cheap trick and can do great harm to real people who are burdened by similar problems.

One of the things that this world can do well without is bigotry in any form. Besides, it won't work. Avoidable physical defects may occasionally be appropriate, although skill based on experience is required to pull it off.

Giving a bad guy stained teeth, halitosis, unkempt hair, or B.O. is entirely different from making him a hairlip.

A pirate with an eye patch and a peg leg is a very old cliche. But it still works because the defects result from the piratic lifestyle.

A fat man with cigar breath and skinned up shins from walking home in the dark after his last KKK meeting is exemplary of the type of physical and character defects that are avoidable by the character. These are what become valuable to the writer who strives to add genuine depth to the beings in his story. But as soon as you also make him a Southern sheriff, you have used an unavoidable trait (his Southerness) to ridicule a stereotype. That ain't fair and it won't work.

On the other hand, poking fun at my co-author Adam is acceptable as he not only deserves ridicule but is truly ridiculous. (The previous sentence represents a test to determine if he is really reading this stuff. If it appears in print we will all know that he was out to lunch instead of working. Regardless, the statement is true.)

If you do decide to use the dossier method, remember to list every conceivable characteristic of each character, no matter how briefly he or she will appear in the story. Expand each list into a dossier' including physical description, preferences, likes and dis-likes, job descriptions, education, relationships with other characters, sexual preferences, and even photos clipped from a catalog. Now the real work begins. An average 'author', keeping his title in mind, writing for his genre, looking occasionally at his notes and guided somewhat by his outline, creates a world in which his well-defined characters participate in eyeball-popping action and use fast paced, appropriate-yet-memorable dialogue so that his readers find it impossible to keep from turning the pages. A few 'authors' have been known to take as much as ten years to do this. (Oh, Gawd.)

Adam

You don't do the plot and then the characters! You make up the characters first!

Then you throw them together and see what they do. You know, how they react to each other and stuff like that.

Do the characters first.

Other than that, Darv said everything I had intended to say. I almost think that he somehow managed to find the notes to this chapter that I seem to have misplaced. Of course if he had, I'm *absolutely certain* that he would have returned them.

Except for that one glaring error concerning the order in which to create characters and plot, Darv has said everything exactly as I would have, word for word. Of course some writers do actually write the characters and the plot at about the same time, developing both at once, but they are wrong to do so, in my humble yet highly accurate opinion.

Stealing notes is wrong too.

6
PLOT

What is plot?

Plot is action, what the characters, the Gods, the fates, the unknown, the environment, or the society do. The main thrust of using plot in stories and novels consists of grabbing the reader's attention and holding on for dear life.

Beware! Story lines and burial sites are both called "plots".

Non-writers seem always to marvel at the ability of an author to dream up a story, and yet for most writers, it is the easiest task in building a good piece of work. Naturally, spy thrillers and mysteries rely heavily on intricate plots for their appeal, but most stories are fairly simple.

Character, dialogue, style, and technique are ever the more difficult tasks.

There is one school of thought that teaches there are only nine basic plots anyway. They are Man vs Man, Man vs Himself, Man vs God, Man vs Fate, Man vs The Unknown, Man vs The Machine, Man vs Nature, Man vs Circumstances, and Man vs Society. (We would add a tenth—Man vs Money.) According to this school of thought, the crux of writing is not to create a new plot - because you're beaten before you start - but to tell the same old plots in new ways. Subplots are brought in to add interesting twists and depth.

The cliche regarding plot today is "show, don't tell".

Two examples follow:

'She seduced him' would be telling.

Showing is done like this: 'Her hot breath fused with his and her long nails trailed thin crimson lines down his back as she pulled him into her bed.' Break time.

The phrase 'he raped her' is telling.

Showing would be, 'Gripping her arm, he spun her around. Her terrified scream was cut short as the chunk of pipe he held smashed into her jaw. His large gloved fist caught her thin blouse, ripping it away as she fell.' Get the idea?

Years ago, in deference to the sensitivity of readers, authors used words such as struck, released, cried, ran after, consumed, bled, took, fainted, forcefully closed, fired, and deflowered in their respective places. Today these words are uncool.

They have been replaced with such words as belted, threw, screamed, chased, devoured, blew apart, wrenched, passed out, slammed, shot, screwed, and the 'F' word to show action.

Many authors obviously feel their greatest creative calling is in making the most shocking use of existing words - or in creating words where existing ones aren't shocking enough.

We once heard a five year old boy, who was angry with his father, call Dad a 'weenex'. What a great new word!

Justification is made through the explanation that reading is in direct competition with television. That modern technology has created television sets small enough to be worn as wristwatches seems to be the crux of the argument. Additionally, remote television control, with its speedy channel changing ability, has resulted in the belief that the typical attention span in this country is slightly less than five seconds.

These myths are so outrageous we feel obligated to debunk them immediately. The average portable television weighs 62.7 pounds, a typical paperback book 13.2 ounces. The average set uses 130 watts of increasingly expensive electricity for each hour of playing time. A book uses none. A viewer, pausing long enough to judge his interest level - even on a Saturday afternoon - changes channel at the rate of once in 4.8 seconds. With slight effort, a reader can scan six book titles in the same length of time. Furthermore, try taking your favorite television to the local laundromat or bus stop and see what happens. Not, of course, that it isn't a challenge to read a book when surrounded with cigar smoking men with pictures of evil blue serpents on their biceps and women wearing pink curlers in their hair.

Just as some singers always seem to croon variations of the same melody, some authors use the same plot over and over, relying on different characters, settings, and so forth to individualize their works. In the Cowboy Western genre for example, the plot is usually fairly familiar. If you're old enough (never thought we'd write that!), return to those thrilling days of yesteryear (in front of that new contraption television), and the hearty Hi Ho Silver! In those shows even the dialogue stayed the same.

"Humph, it quiet, Kemosabe," the Indian would say as he sat his horse, always by the same fork in the same trail next to the same boulder.

"Yes, Tonto," replied the Lone Ranger, "Too quiet."

They would ride into town and do The Good Deed; save the distressed damsel, arrest the bad guy or whatever, and ride out again. How incredibly suppressed must have been their sex drives.

In the Sixties, there were forms of entertainment known as Surfer Movies. The plot; boy meets girl, boy gets girl, boy loses girl, boy gets girl back. The titles were different and the color and cut of the swimsuits were different. But the dialogue and the plot and even the actors didn't change. It is interesting to note that the actors chosen were those deemed too old to participate in a television program that starred a large rodent that spoke in a soprano voice. But that has nothing to do with anything discussed here. Breast size of the females was also a factor.

At the other end of the spectrum are Romeo and Juliet and West Side Story. One a story of the children of medieval nobility, the other a story of 1950's street gang members. Each told in its individual and extraordinary way, yet both possessing the same plot.

Often more important than the main plot to overall story quality are the various subplots which are into the work.

Subplots can be used to serve various purposes.

Nancy Neophyte slowly sneaks up the stairs and carefully opens the attic door in chapter seven. The reader's heart is throbbing because chapter six told about the ghost of an evil witch waiting in anticipation of revenge on those who left her, locked in the attic to starve, three hundred years earlier. Subplot heightens reader emotion.

The government has taken over a small town university laboratory. The hero enters carrying a sample of an exotic gas he has risked life and limb to obtain. The gas has come from a meteorite and seems to have a life of its own, floating from town to town, turning all the inhabitants into bleeding leprous carnivorous monsters. Just as the specimen is placed into the test chamber, the cleaning lady saunters in, her mop bucket in tow. She pauses at the center of the room and smiles as she passes wind, setting off all the high tech alarms. Subplot used as humor to relieve tension.

The problem with subplots is they are darned hard to do well. Yet a contemporary novel is comparatively flat without them.

Darv likes to think of subplots as analogous to an addition to a house. Slap a family room to the side of the house and everyone driving by will look at it and say, "Look Marge, the Dimwits have thrown up a family room on the side of their house."

When well done, a house addition looks as if it has been there since the house was built. The roof line blends in, the materials blend or contrast pleasantly, the style of the new mirrors the old, and the landscaping is blended to give an appearance of organic continuity. Thus it should be with subplots. THey should be woven and blended into the main story line. And that takes planning and work.

Adam likes to think of a voluptuous blonde femme fatale preparing a complicated French sauce in his (Adam's) kitchen. The sauce consists of numerous ingredients that must be blended together in a certain way and at a certain temperature, and the blonde is wearing nothing more than a very short apron and a smile. This has nothing whatever to do with subplots, plots, or even writing, he just likes to think of it.

Whether you choose to develop an intricate and challenging main plot which carries the story along, or a simple plot interwoven with intricate and challenging subplots, or some hybrid, an outline is essential. Without an outline you are likely to end up with something that reads like a Dick and Jane story narrated by Henry Kissinger.

One of the authors has written a spectacularly unsuccessful novel without benefit of a sufficiently thorough outline.

The book opens in a snowstorm. In a later chapter (two weeks hence in the story) the main character is sitting in his car watching a young girl practice diving into a swimming pool. Even though a young person can be credited with a hearty constitution and weather can change rapidly in most of the country, credibility was stretched a tad. Picture a Sumo wrestler putting on PeeWee Herman's jacket.

The problem was resolved by putting the girl into a sweatsuit and having her practice on a trampoline. The point is that such details can mess up a story badly.

An author may spend months or years creating a story. Memory for most of us is just not quite perfect. Without the guiding force of a concise outline, mistakes of this nature can happen. Mistakes an avid reader will find in a matter of hours. One of the authors read a novel by Agatha Christie in which five feet of snow fell one day and the next day crocuses were blooming.

Here is a technique that may help.

Start by making an overall general outline. Divide a page into three columns. In the first column list the things you want to happen, the plot and subplots. Next to each, write down the characters involved in the second column. In the third column, you can put the settings, locations, etc. across from the story actions. Use the fourth column for any miscellaneous notes that will help in the next step. (What? You say we told you to start with only three columns? Now you know what happens without an organized outline, don't you!)

Number the entries in your first column in the order you'd like them to occur in your story. Get a clean sheet of paper and rewrite your lists in order. Now draw horizontal lines between your entries about where you think the chapters should begin and end.

The next step is to outline the first chapter in as much detail as you can. Outline the second in some detail and rough in the third. Now you're ready to write the first chapter.

When you're done, go back and re-outline the second chapter in extreme detail. This will probably change due to developments that occurred while you were writing chapter one. Perhaps a character struck your fancy and will require a little extra something to develop. Or you may have discovered a slight twist of plot or change in timing that you hadn't seen before.

Redo the outline for chapter three in greater detail next, referring to your master outline. Follow this by roughing in chapter four.

Now write chapter two. When complete, rewrite the outline for chapters three, four, and five. Follow the pattern until your novel is finished.

Following this procedure will keep your story flowing, your characters in line, and will help you remember the details.

This way, when you complete your work and submit it to a publisher, you will sell it on the first try, and without all those nasty rewrite requirements. This is a lie, of course. Its just that if you had known how much work is involved, you might have been turned off without a little encouragement.

Because there is so darned much work involved in this method of plot development, we feel obligated to tell you how to come up with a blockbuster (okay, at least an acceptable) plot a whole lot easier. So here goes.

Get a pencil and paper and plunk yourself down in front of the television. If you are looking for a strong plot, write down everything that happens during the program. This assumes, of course that the tube is turned on. If not, turn it on. If you want a story that has intertwined subplots, copy what happens during the commercials, too. When you write your novel, remember to change the characters, settings, and at least some of the dialogue.

Don't worry that the publisher's editor will catch on. Editors, hard working dedicated people that they are, never watch television.

7
DIALOGUE

Dialogue is what appears in cartoon balloons. It is used by 'real' writers for more that just having their dossier'ed characters, or the Aunt Bertha model, talk among themselves. There seems to be no magic formula to determine the ratio of narrative to dialogue. It is supposed to add something called depth.

Many writers are wary of using dialogue, but it is a skill easily learned with practice. As in any part of writing, you must think before you ink. What is it you wish to convey? What is the best way to convey it, narrative, dialogue, or pictures? Where can dialogue be used to provide humor, punctuation, shock, drama, or color? Balloons over the heads of characters in cartoons solve the toughest problem in writing dialogue, that is how to identify and track who is saying what. One often used alternative in books is that of identifying only the first of two speakers. It is a cheap trick but it works, if it doesn't cover so many pages that the reader has to start over when reopening the book after starting the laundry, answering the phone, yelling at the neighbor's dog for squatting in the front yard, or reminding the kids for the eighteenth time to turn the damned television down. Here's an example:

Sue yelled, "Hey Bob, is that you?"
"Yes."

"Where have you been?"

"In the basement."

"What were you doing down there?"

"Reading a magazine."

"What magazine?"

"Never mind, get your hind end in here and fasten my necklace for me."

"I don't wear necklaces."

"I know that! You're Bob, remember? And I'm Sue doing the talking now."

"Right, I got confused there for a moment."

"Okay, forget it. You may have noticed that I am whispering now."

"Yes I did."

"And I am speaking melodiously."

"Indeed you are. Can you empty the garbage now?"

"Am I Sue or am I Bob? Sue thinks that garbage dumping is man's work. So if I am Sue, I don't do garbage."

"You're Bob."

"Right. I'll empty the garbage. I'm sure you can hear that I'm answering with a note of resignation in my voice."

Through the use of dialogue, characters describe each other, show emotion, advance the plot, and describe portions of the setting. Rather than simply telling the reader that Joe had a giant, ugly mole on his bottom lip, Mary says, "Joe, you have a giant, ugly mole on your bottom lip."

Better yet Sally (another character in the story) says, "Mary, have you noticed that Joe has a giant, ugly mole on his bottom lip?"

Dialogue is used to show emotion, like this:

"Hi Mary, I'm Joe."

"AAARGH!"

Here's how dialogue is used to advance the story and

describe the setting, too.

Joe says, "I jutht don't underthtand, I took Mary out to the nithesht rethtaurant in town and all she could do wath thtare at my faith."

(See the section of the chapter "Characters" concerning ridicule of physical defects. It is this kind of confusion that occurs when a book is co-authored. Both authors have agreed to leave this paragraph intact as a dramatic demonstration of both the advance-the-story and the don't-ridicule-handicaps points.)

Writing dialogue of characters who speak with accents, also known as dialect, is another matter entirely. Just as there are few people who can effectively tell jokes with dialect (Did you hear the one about the Irishman who rolled over in bed one morning and said to his wife . . .) There are few who can write it effectively, unless it is their own. A Yankee trying to write the haggling of Billy Bob Beauregard Pikkins while he horse-trades with a Union soldier is as tough as a Texan creating the sparse commentary of a Maine guide lost in the North woods. It can be done but it takes practice.

Reading it aloud is the acid test.

Warning!

Reading colloquial dialogue aloud while alone in your writing room may lead your family to have you committed to an institution where there is no paper and you are denied anything as sharp as a pencil. Thus the untimely end of an otherwise brilliant writing career. Just as difficult as dialect is the task of writing the thoughts of a character as dialogue.

To wit:

Emily paused at the crest of the small hill, leaning against the staff she always carried to fend off the dogs.

"Gosh," she thought, "what a lovely day!" She sat and,

straightening her skirt, continued her musing.

"This is just wonderful. I'm such a lucky girl. There won't be many more days as nice as this." She smiled.

"Winter is just around the corner. I am so lucky to be alive. And to be the only person on God's earth who talks to herself in whole, but otherwise flawed, sentences."

Nearly everyone is familiar with the adage "actions speak louder than words". In writing, where this translates to "narrative says more than dialogue", the theory is not necessarily true. Dialogue can be much more economical than description. Say for example that you wanted to establish that Amos was intolerant of mosquitoes. You could create a scene exemplifying that attitude by having Amos dancing around the room, slapping himself and spraying the air with Raid and possibly buckshot and using three or more pages doing it. Or, you could do it this way.

"Amos, you seem so suddenly remote, dear," Margaret whispered from her side of the bed.

"Sorry, it isn't you," he replied. "Its these darned mosquitoes. I hate them."

Of course there are exceptions.

Rex paused momentarily, reflecting on the jeering insults of the other man.

"Violence has never been a part of my life. And yet I am certain that I could overpower you," he told his adversary. "You are much older than I, smaller, and you're wheezing badly."

He turned.

"Would it be best to walk away from this?" he asked his girlfriend, who was still tied to the cookstove. "To extricate myself from this confrontation and risk losing the girl of my dreams, as well as the treasure? Or to forge ahead, as they say, into hitherto unknown realms, ignoring the possibly irreversible harm to my own sense of self-worth."

"Let us consider, Rex," answered the girl. "The consequences must be weighed."

The other man put his hands to his ears and went to his knees. "Please!" he blurted weakly. "I can't stand this! Take the treasure - and the girl. Just shut up and get out!"

Compare that to the following:

Rex hit the man hard on the side of the head with a pipewrench, knocking him cold. He cut the girl's bonds, freeing her from the cookstove, and together they grabbed up the treasure and went to Sri Lanka.

Use of dialogue is also handy if you have an overwhelming urge to cuss. Your mother would certainly frown should the "F" word happen to slip from your mouth. But if one of your characters has the habit of using words that would bring a blush to the face of a sailor, you might get away with it.

Another risk you run in writing dialogue is that, at least at first, all of the characters will talk just like you. Remember Joe Friday on Dragnet? After listening to a half-hour program, even Dan Akroid would talk like him. In order to avoid this, you must have your character so well formed in your mind you can not only see but hear him or her.

In the chapter on characters (not intended to be an autobiographical term), two methods for visualizing a character are suggested. One is the creation of a detailed dossier, the other being the choosing of a real-life person as a model. Either method is effective in drawing your own characters, each has inherent strengths and weaknesses. Yet the real-life method is superior in determining manner of speech. If you use the dossier method, you may wish, at least in the beginning of your career, to note the manners of speech of people a little more in the public eye.

"Hey there, tall, dark and handsome. When this chapter is over, come on up and see me sometime."

"You can bet on it, Pilgrim."

How to Develop Dialogue the Hard Way

Read everything ever written by William Shakespeare, Ernest Hemingway, Will Rogers, Mark Twain and Dr. Seuss.

Locate and listen to every recording you can get your hands on of Oliver North's Senate Subcommittee testimony, Mr. Roger's Neighborhood, and Motel 6 commercials.

Memorize Webster's Unabridged Dictionary, 2nd edition, the Encyclopedia Britannica, and the Torah.

Pretend that you are sending a letter to Mom (yours, not ours) and start writing.

How to Develop Thrilling Blockbuster Dialogue the Easy Way

Get a tape recorder.
Put a tape in it.
Put it on top of your television.
Turn it on to "record".
Turn your television on.
Wait ten to fifteen seconds.
Change the channel.
Wait ten or fifteen seconds again.
Repeat until the tape stops.
Rewind the tape and copy everything you have recorded word for word, even the commercials. (Remember to change the names, though.)

You now have not only created vivid dialogue that will be easily recognized by millions of television viewers across the country, you also have a number of simultaneously occurring plots!

It's foolproof.

If you are fortunate enough to run across reruns of I Love Lucy or The Dick VanDyke Show, so much the better. Mayberry, RFD is the gem of gems.

Keep in mind, too, that the words you have just copied were originally written by some of the most highly paid writers in the world.

8

RESEARCH

Research is the cold, wet, hairy hand of fear that reaches out from the darkest corner of your grandmother's basement, way back behind the old oil furnace, where the coal bin used to be.

The word reminds many a writer of an assignment forced upon him/her by a Junior High School teacher. A shudder passes through the author. If the assignment, usually called a Research Project or Term Paper or something similarly frightening, was ever completed, the grade never seemed to be higher than a C-.

"Real" writers can spend years researching material for a novel, and merrily deduct trips to Bulgaria to study bulgur and to Louisiana to study grits as they do so.

Worry not, dear reader! We will show you how to breeze through this aspect of authoring, too. But first, as always, we must show you how them what does it does it.

What is research? Research consists of hours upon hours upon hours spent reading moldy history books, dusty old manuscripts and diaries, crumbling letters, ancient maps, and tombstones. The researcher talks to old college professors, visits stuffy museums, and just wanders around in the least populated parts of libraries, county records departments, and churches. A thoroughly boring and very time consuming practice.

We would be remiss, however, if we did not acknowledge the thrill of discovery that occasionally ignites the brain of the researcher. Picture an egg laid by a cackling hen, squatting in the rafters.

Authors do this research ostensibly in order to provide their readers with historical accuracy, or at least a barely conscious but authentic feeling of the time and place in which their story occurs.

See the chapter entitled SETTING. Go ahead. We'll wait.

Can't find it? Want to know why? It is not really a chapter, it is disguised as part of another chapter. Look again. Consider it a small exercise in research. Fun, isn't it.

In reality, research is an attempt to gain extensions on loans or get increases in the advancements from publishers. The ploy seldom works, but it might fool your spouse or special friend enough to let you take one more day off your real job.

Authors take, make, and keep notes. Lots of notes. It would seem that they see themselves as literary amoeba, living on —indeed consuming— vast amounts of information and leaving behind files, stacks, and shoeboxes full of notes. The notes are occasionally organized into outlines. This is the means through which authors appear to assemble their notes into rough patterns of sorts. It supposedly helps them keep the characters in their stories from jumping all over Creation and back. Please note this statement does not necessarily apply to novels written in the Fantasy or Science Fiction genres.

Sounds like a royal pain in the old patootie, doesn't it? You're right, it is. Can you become a rich and famous author without it? Of course you can. Lots of people already have.

BUT, we are sure that there are a FEW of you out there who

MIGHTreally want to do research. You know who you are. You're those Salutatorians and Valedictorians who can't get along without doing everything just exactly right. Please don't think we are making fun of you. Some of our best friends are firstborns.

Let us assume for a moment that you really lust to do research for your book. A few suggestions may be helpful. Don't forget, if you get tired of it you can always pitch it and move on to our foolproof method to beat the system.

Okay, you literary perfectionists out there, listen up. There have been many books written on how to do research and how to organize it once you've done it. We'd suggest that you buy or borrow one or two and read them. We expect that, being the perfectionist you are, you no doubt already have. So go read a couple more.

Anyone can, in ten or fifteen minutes, learn the basics of either the Dewey Decimal or Library of Congress system of library organization by going to a library and using it.

If you have a problem with either of these systems, try the Huey or Louie Decimal systems.

If all else fails, you can play the often forgotten game Ask The Librarian. Librarians, with very few exceptions, are quiet, polite and helpful people. In fact, librarians have gained the general reputation of being too dull to include as subjects in any modern novel, but whose thumbprints are often found in profusion on the edges of the seamiest novels.

From here it is best to break research into two parts, research for historical novels and research for contemporary works. The suggestions that follow are those that we see as being in addition to what one would typically find in a typical "How To Do Research" kind of book.

Historical Research

Technically, if you write about something that happened

yesterday, you are writing in a historical mode, or in an historical mode, depending on preference. We are going to assume, however, that the term historical refers to things that happened at least one hundred years ago. We are also going to assume that you have already picked the general timeframe and location for your work.

Big Time Writing Hint Thrown In At No Extra Charge

If it is explained well, a fiction writer can assume almost anything. Now, to work.

First, read a modern history of your chosen time and place.

Second, read an account of the same place written during the time you have chosen.

Third, compare the two for author bias.

Fourth, purchase music written in the setting you have chosen. Sheet music is fine if you can play the piano, but a CD performed by a bunch of eggheads with lutes and recorders would be better.

Fifth, listen to the CD as you write.

Sixth, obtain a costume dated from your chosen time and general geographical area.

Seventh, wear it as you write.

Eighth, rent movies matching your chosen setting.

Ninth, watch the movies, but not as you write. You can, if you wish, wear your costume while you watch, but draw your drapes first.

Tenth, date a librarian and persuade him/her/her/him to do your research for you in all her/his/his/her spare time.

CAUTIONS:

1. If you happen to be married, the previous step is a dangerous one and can be deleted if absolutely necessary.

2. Don't wear your costume on your dates.

Contemporary Research

First, read everything you can get your hands on.

Second, listen to every conversation that you can. Yes, eavesdrop.

Third, take notes. Or not, depending on your mood.

Fourth, arrange a radio so that it will play an all-news station throughout the night as you sleep. It needn't be in your bedroom because that subliminal stuff doesn't work anyway. It sounds mystical and will impress your friends. Do not listen to late-night comedy/talk shows. In the event that subliminal persuasion really does work, your writing will be loaded with cliches, penis references and dumb jokes.

Fifth, ask questions. Ask as many as you can think of the instant that you think of them, from anyone within earshot.

Sixth, watch as much television as you can in the time remaining. This won't help your research a bit, but everybody needs the occasional break.

CAUTION:

If you are married, you won't get away with doing much of this stuff for very long either, so work fast.

BEATING THE SYSTEM

For those thousands of you who get goose bumps just thinking about doing research, follow these easy steps.

Historical Research

First, obtain a book written in or around the time period chosen for your novel.

Second, create a list of old words used in the book and their contemporary counterparts. Here is a brief list as an example:

Thee or Thou	- You
Hearken	- Yo, Dude!
Verily	- Sure
Sayeth	- Said
Unto	- To, at, or with
Smitten	- Done went and got smacked
Besmirched	- Got dragged through the mud
Vapors	- Fart
Depredations	- We don't know, but it is impressive. Use it a lot.
Brakish	- Came from a guy named Brak
Codpiece	- Jock strap
Lo!	- Hey
Skullery	- Dishwasher
Foresworn	- Cussed
Chaste	- Very unpopular but clean
Prithee	- Outhouse
Farthing	- Something very distant

Now, write your book in modern language. Run the old words through the "Search and Replace" function of your word processor, exchanging the new with the old.

Contemporary Research

The best advise we can give you concerning research for writing a modern novel is this.

Don't.

Now, you say, is that any way to be? There you sit, staring at this page with a frustration smirk on your facebones, thinking that we authors are copping out of giving you real help and trying too hard to pull off another stupid joke. We aren't joking. Not this time.

Today's Americans are exposed to more transactions of information in a single day than our grandparents were in a fortnight (another old word). In other words, most of us are in a state of info-overload. So why do research when the real challenge is to slow down the stuff coming in long enough to write.

Don't believe us? Go look it up.

A Final Note On Research

Footnotes and bibliographies are essential in scholarly works but pompous in novels. Research should melt into your work like sugar into batter, leaving no trace of the gritty granules but sweetening the cake.

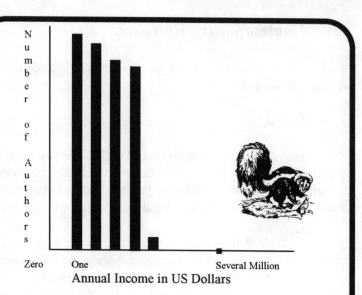

Number of Authors

Zero   One   Several Million

Annual Income in US Dollars

78

9

GRAPHICS

Any publication can be dressed up through the effective use of graphics.

Graphics are photographs, drawings, illustrations, charts, graphs, borders, and so forth. Graphics are not the coffee stains or jelly donut drippings on your manuscript, unless of course they bear resemblance to one of your characters. Then again, if your main character happens to be a coffee swilling jelly donut fanatic, it might lend a little realism.

Graphics can be broken down into two categories, internal (between the covers) and external (on the cover). Rules for use vary according to the type of book. Here are a few examples to help you understand the concept.

Autobiographies

By law all autobiographies are required to display photos of the author. These photos must show the author shooting pheasants, shaking hands (and smiling) with a President (preferably a living one) or popular foreign leader, dandling a child on one knee, or receiving an award. All facial expressions must be such that sincerity oozes from every pore. So if you are thinking about your autobiography and don't already have photos which exactly meet these criteria, don't write it.

Military Books

Also by law, all books about military campaigns -real or fictional- must display a battlefield map. If the book is published in hardcover, the map must be glued to the inside of the front cover. For paperbacks, it can be anywhere, but style points are taken off if it is easy to find. Points are also removed according to legibility. The harder the map is to decipher, the better. The only exception to the above is if you are a recently unemployed military cartographer forced to work nights writing your autobiography to pay off the lawsuit brought against you by the ASPCA (American Society of Pheasant Cruelty Avoidance). In your case, aerial photographs are permitted.

Scientific Works

Tables, charts and graphs are most commonly used in non-fiction books. Since people who buy such books either study the graphics or read the text - but never both -accuracy is not important. Scientists, especially economists, begin a display of every new topic with tables; just as some fiction writers start each chapter with a verse or two of some obscure poetry nobody ever reads. Other scientific writers decorate their works with charts and graphs. The graphs are either a line that runs up or down and from left to right with unexplained numbers along the vertical and horizontal legs or a two-page spread loaded with multicolored lines of various textures and innumerable footnotes. Any useful information is printed in the crease between the pages.

Obviously nothing in between is permitted and the drier the better. And the more tables, charts and graphs the better. Since most science books contain only three paragraphs of genuine text, graphics are a real necessity. In fact, as five-pound tomes sell better than three-inch paragraphs, charts and such are enthusiastically encouraged.

Romances, Gothic

Here is the best way to reinforce what we are about to tell you concerning Gothic Romance graphics. Go to a store that specializes in such books, your local supermarket or discount drugstore. Go to the check-out counter. Find the racks right next to the tabloid newspapers that scream headlines of UFO-born chicken-headed babies grinding their mothers up in garbage disposals because God told them to, and there you are. You are presently standing before a mind-boggling array of Gothic Romances. When you've finished boggling, look closely.

Did you ever know that there are so many shades of mauve? There are other less obvious characteristics shared by all of this kind of book. They have to do with the background and the foreground. The background will always contain a ship, battlefield, opulent bedroom, or burning mansion. The foreground will always contain a man and a woman.

The woman will:
1) be large of breast
>A) showing through a wet and storm-torn blouse
>or
>B) thrusting up as if to burst over the confines of a bodice.
2) have hair either auburn, raven, vermilion, or peroxide-flaxen in hue
>A) blowing in the wind or
>B) cascading across the chest of her man.

The man will:
1) be dark and swarthy or
2) be blond and ruddy.
3) wear a military uniform or
4) bear a slight but strategically placed scar on his face.

They will be posed so that:
1) The woman looks up at the man from right to left or
2) The woman looks up at the man from left to right.

81

3) Only if injured may the man look up at the woman.

Romances, Western

Western romances are found either just below the Gothics or on the other side of the tabloid rack. The background will always contain a ship, battlefield, opulent bedroom, or burning log cabin.

The men may wear buckskin. Otherwise the covers are the same as the Gothic Romances, except the man may look up at the horse.

Surprisingly or unsurprisingly as the case may be, the covers of these kinds of books have never been subjected to the scrutiny of modern science. Should this become the case, science will come to two startling conclusions.

First, that there had evolved no racial minorities, especially Blacks and Asians, prior to the historical periods portrayed. A tiny sampling of Native Americans may have been present, in the form of growths on the backs of spotted ponies.

And second, since these minorities do presently exist and are equivalent if not superior in capabilities to the majority of society today, it is only reasonable to conclude that their obviously accelerated rate of evolution will catapult them into cultural superiority before the end of this month.

The most obvious use of graphics, and primary attention-getting (read 'selling') feature is the book's cover.

Consider for example the obvious care and expense given to the jacket of this book.

The quality of which it speaks no doubt played a large part in getting your attention and in leading to your purchase. The photo was Darv's doing. Following his solid get-it-right-the-first-time philosophy, he wisely took a number of pictures of a hot-pink church on the way to the photo session, making the cover photo the last

82

picture on the roll. Giving credit to the photographer or artist is also very important from both moral and legal perspectives.

Many thanks to our artiste professionale, Some Guy in a Lawn Chair.

Actually, the only genuine use of interior graphics as we see it is to fill pages when your publisher informs you that your Great Work isn't quite great enough.

EDITOR'S NOTE:

As you may have noticed, the cover design has been changed, with that of Our Authors placed elsewhere. This was the result of yet another day-long discussion. *(I hate seeing grown men cry - and this time the replacement of my furniture comes out of their pockets!)*

10
PROOFREADING

Proofreading is synonymous with rewriting. Face it, if you or someone else is going to read your manuscript for proof that it contains no mistakes -and you or they find one- you're going to have to rewrite some of it anyway. Maybe.

Why didn't we title this chapter Rewriting instead? Because we harp about rewriting so darned much throughout this book that, frankly, we were a bit concerned that you might be tempted to skip this chapter. So, grab your lyres and listen to our harping. As a consolation, this is a short chapter.

REWRITING

This is the step where writers go over every word of the book they have just finished. They cut or replace words, paragraphs, pages, and even whole chapters. For some reason, nobody seems to be able to get it right the first time.

MORE REWRITING

This is done because writers never seem to be happy with the results of their earlier efforts. Also, more times than not, the big ugly mole that was on Joe's top lip in your novel (See the chapter on Dialogue.) has, by chapter twelve, managed to move to his bottom lip.

STILL MORE REWRITING

Once in a purple-and-green-plaid-with-orange-polka-dots moon, an agent accepts a new writer's manuscript. Sort of. The polite "You gotta be joking" sticky-note is replaced with a full-size page. Hidden among all the flowery verbiage is the statement, "Your work might be publishable if . . ." The agent will then proceed to ask that the first half of the work be rewritten and the second half replaced.

EVEN MORE REWRITING

Even more rarely, the manuscript gets into the hands of an editor. Should a writer ever hear from one, and should it relate to the possible acceptance of his manuscript, and should it happen to be the manuscript the agent has finally accepted, the dialogue will no doubt be as follows: "Call me after you have replaced the first half and rewritten the second and we'll talk about it." Be prepared, rewriting will take anywhere from two to several thousand times as long as the original effort. If rewriting were perfume, it would be called "Eau d'boring".

PROOFREADING

Face it, the fewer mistakes in your manuscript, the easier it will be to read. Grab your Handy-Dandy Dictionary (This is not an endorsement.) and look up every word, phrase, and punctuation mark you aren't 101% sure about. If you can't stand the thought of this task, write westerns, and do the entire book in dialectical dialogue. Hain't sich a bad idear, hey?

STILL EVEN MORE REWRITING?

'Fraid so, pard. Now its time to fix all those grammar, punctuation, and spelling errors. Don't worry if you don't find or correct them all. Only the editar and your mither will catch the ones you missed. More than one great writer has admitted to rewriting the same sentence over forty times. Unfortunately, the names escape us at the moment. Probably dead now anyway. Terminal keyboard cramps.

BEAT IT!

How? Don't correct a damn thing.

Instead, if someone should happen to speak up about having a little difficulty reading your masterwork, put a deeply insulted look on your face, look him straight in the face, and repeat after me . . .

"This, my dear (editor, reader, critic, mother) happens to be nothing less than the finest example of free-form poetry of this or any previous century. I assure you that every mark, every symbol, has been individually agonized over. Nothing, I repeat nothing, have I left to the vagaries of doubt or chance. Although some things may at first appear to be mistakes, they are not. They're placed in such a way that the reader's sensitivities are heightened as related to the emotions portrayed here. Indeed, heightened beyond levels previously thought to be humanly possible. I've asked you to read it knowing that the only requirement of the reader is a vastly superior intellect combined with a small amount of compassion for the strains of genius involved in the creation of a 180,000 word poem and the leap of faith and trust made in allowing you to be the first to enjoy this piece."

A word of caution, try not to be cleaning your navel of lint as you recite it. An editor, a reader, or critic won't fall for this. Your mom won't either, but at least she'll act as if she does.

11
PSEUDONYMS

Pseudonyms, or pen names, are names that writers use when their own won't do.

Historically pseudonyms were attached to political or economic tracts that ran contrary to the ideas or beliefs enforced by kings or dictators. Many times pen names were used literally to save their authors' necks.

Today the reasons may not be as critical. However, they are more numerous. Authors use phony names to hide themselves from creditors, ex-spouses, ex-lovers, and the attorneys of people who claim to have been libeled. Phony monikers have also been used by writers in attempts to enhance their chances of selling books.

You may wish to use a phony name, for whatever reason. Perhaps your parents cursed you with Earnest Hemingway Jones or Emily Dickinson Smith. Maybe you just feel that your name is not attractive to the ear or eye. As a parallel example, compare "phony name" with "pseudonym" or "nom de plume".

Maybe your given name lacks the punch that could drive your book into the bestseller category.

Consider, for example, which of these two names gives the potential purchaser the greater vision of the ruggedness of the American cowboy; Max Brand or Louis L'Amour. One sounds like a rawhide-clad fist smashing into a lean jawbone. The other could be the logo for a line of purple designer tights. If anyone were foolish enough to write westerns under the name of Louis L'Amour, she or he would surely fail.

It could be that you don't want your mother-in-law to learn that her favorite S&M porno novel was written by her youngest son's wife. Maybe you are a retired Marine Corps drill sergeant-turned professional wrestler and you don't want to upset Mamma (or the boys at the bar) with your name plastered across the cover of a sexless-but-touching Southern Belle romance. In the past, men have written under female aliases and women under male aliases, with the belief that his or her gender at birth may be a hindrance to sales.

According to a very old survey, most people have sex organs, and nine times out of ten, those organs are male or female. (One time out of ten they are Wurlitzer.) Change gender when writing and the next thing you know, men will be wearing long hair, women will cut theirs short, they will start wearing each other's clothes and nobody will be able to tell them apart! Men will start doing housework and discussing sensitivity! Women will begin doing "traditionally male" jobs and demanding equal pay! The whole fabric of our society will rend! Or worse—it may tear.

Suffice to say that using a pseudonym normally attributed to the opposite gender is not recommended. Whatever your reason, if you do decide to use a fake name, don't get cute. Yes, it worked for Samuel Clemens.

But please review the following examples, asking yourself,"Would I purchase this book by this author?"

Who Shot Amy Collenstein?
by Trip Hammer and Dee Butler

Colonic Itching
by Royd Hemmor

The Double Red Rose
by Rose Redd

Carrier Attack
by A. Harrier

Fixed At The Polls
by U. Nanimous

Horseshoe Haven
by V. Lage Smithy

The Hazards Of Religious Fervor
by Hue Sein

Curing Baldness
by Harry Butts

Collectible Ceramics
by Clay Potter

The only exception is that you can use any name you wish if you are writing a Gothic Romance. The cover illustration is the only thing that matters.

Certain names seem to breed success. MacDonald, for example. John, Ross, and Gregory MacDonald (or McDonald) all hit the big leagues in the same century. If you want to follow suit, check the card catalog at your local library and steal a good, hearty, successful name, one with a proven track record. Rushdie comes to mind if you like danger.

Much of the choice of a pen name will have to do with the genre you choose. Penelope Persimmon may work well for a book on the weaving of sewing baskets, but not so well on the cover of a monograph about re-roofing barns.

Spike McFall would be a great name for the next Jack London. Yet some might find it a trifle intimidating printed beneath the title of an article on cuticle removal in 'Podiatry Week' magazine.

If you do go for a pseudonym, be warned that certain dilemmas may present themselves. If you are not confident of your earliest works, an alias is just the ticket to protect your family from the scoffing and jeering of friends and neighbors. But what if you hit it big?

Your first book sells a million copies. Euphoric, you hurry off on business and get stopped for speeding. You see that the policeman has a copy of your book sticking out of his pocket (small book/large Sam Brown pocket).

"So, Mr. Simone Bratslavski, you goin' to a fire or sumpin?"

"No, officer," you reply, a confident smirk playing about your lips, "I'm heading to the book store to autograph some copies of my latest book. By the way, I see you have a copy there. I'll be happy to sign it for you."

At this point you will most likely receive one of two possible reactions.

"Excuse me, Mr. B. Simone, I didn't realize. Gee what a nifty idea, switching your first and last names like that. How witty. Yes, please autograph my book. Put down "To my buddy Burt, all the best." Oh, heavens, Mr. Simone, I wouldn't think of ticketing you. Just a friendly reminder. That's B-u-r-t, with a capital "B".

OR

"Ha! You think I'm gonna believe for a minute that Ned

Nightstick is really a balding old fart wearin' an old brown suit an' a stained yellow tie! Outa the car, Turkey! Assume da position!"

The best place to seek advise about your choice of a pseudonym is with your publisher. Of course, if you don't have a memorable, catchy name you may never find a publisher.

The worst place to seek such advise is from your mother. After all, if she hadn't screwed up your real name, you wouldn't be in this predicament.

Our advise to you is always use your real name. It is the only honest way to conduct your writing career.

By the way, both of this book's authors are using aliases.

Mr. Harfield once got caught as a teenager "doing donuts" on a deserted snow covered airstrip. The best name he could think of in such a pinch was Darvin P. Harfield. He has since written under that name (If this is being read by a tax examiner, we are just kidding.) although he prefers to be called Darv, thinking that Darvin is a bit stuffy.

Mr. Poszar is a gypsy who prefers exotic name such as Zoltan the Seer and a currently unemployed part-time CIA agent and Army Intelligence officer in real life. By the way, he denies all this vehemently.

Coincidentally, both have been referred to by various publishers as Rejection Slip Enclosed. This is believed to be an ancient Druidic holy name.

The true coincidence is in how both names are derived from the same Druidic phrase. This speaks volumes about the variance in translations of Druidic texts.

12
AGENTS, EDITORS, PUBLICATION, ETC.

The steps involved in the writing for publication of any work are normally as follows:

1. Creation. Dream up a story.
2. Writing. Self explanatory. Obvious, too.
3. Rewriting. Twice. Thrice. And again until YOU JUST CAN'T STAND TO DO IT AGAIN AND IF YOU HAVE TO YOU WILL START DROOLING AND SCREAMING AND RIPPING THE HAIR FROM YOU HEAD *AAAARRRGGGGHHHHHHHH!!!!!!!!*
4. Editing. Finding somebody to tell you how to fix it.
5. More Rewriting. Fixing what the editor claimed was "incorrect". (Sigh)
6. Agenting. Finding somebody to sell it.
7. Additional Rewriting. One more stinking time, for the agent, that pathetic son of a flea bitten myopic bag lady.

8. Publisher's Editor. Finding somebody to print it.

9. Even More Rewriting. Grit your teeth, buy a bottle of moonshine, hire a divorce lawyer and a financial consultant, attend psychotherapy, and rewrite the rotten, lousy, stinking oppressive thing again, usually in the quiet sanctum of a neoprene lined room.

Steps 1 and 2 are pieces of Gramma Bradislavski's sweetbread.

Step 4 is also easy. The editor must be someone who has the courage to be honestly and constructively critical. This step is easier still if you are married or have a mother who can read.

A background in martial arts is also helpful.

Steps 3, 5, 7, and 9 can be a trifle onerous. All we can say is that you must strive to achieve the level of mental stability of a piece of Indiana limestone.

This brings us to the discussion of steps 6 and 8, the primary subjects of this chapter. These items will be discussed in the next sections. Publication will be discussed in a later section. The one to three sections after have been included for your additional understanding, with a final section containing even more comments. Don't worry, all sections are labeled with Roman numerals for clarity.

Part I (Roman for Part 1)
AGENTS

Agents are people who make their living by battling day and night to:

Protect their clients from all the evil editors out there in Publisher Land.

Negotiate fair, equitable and honest contracts for their author clients.

Decipher, explain, modify, and re-explain contracts between publisher and author.

Make arrangements for tours and conferences so that authors can push their books.

Handle the royalty checks from publishers, assuring that they are of the correct amount and arrive on time to the author.

All this for a mere pittance, anywhere from ten to thirty-five per cent of the monies paid to the author. All the sleepless nights *(If I want you to get my book published I'm going to have to do WHAT?)*, hard work *(Let's have lunch tomorrow and we'll discuss it.)*, and fast-paced lifestyle *(I've got to go to Acapulco for a couple of weeks to check on the potential movie rights.)* do, however, put a bit of a strain on agents.

This is why agents have begun charging what is known as **reading fees**. Reading fees are charges made to writers "to defray the exorbitant administrative and service costs incurred." by the agents. The best explanation is through a description of the typical experience of the typical writer trying to sell his or her first book.

The first-time writer, being an honest person, thinks that in order to sell a book he or she must first have a book to sell. This person then spends a year or two creating, writing, researching, rewriting, and so forth. Now it must be sold. But who will sell it? Why not an agent? They're nice honest people and they must be good at it, it's what they do for a living. So the writer looks through a variety of sources and comes up with a list of names of literary agents. He or she then sends out from five to nine letters explaining who she/he is, why she/he wrote this book, why the book will become a bestseller, and so forth. And he or she waits.

In a couple of months or so, most of the replies will have come in. They will be polite, courteous, and professional. Most of them will say "no", "you must be kidding" or something similar.

Invariably one will say something to the effect of, "Your book shows promise. It may even be publishable. If so, we predict that you could see a sizable advance within a few short weeks of our sale of your manuscript."

"Unfortunately, our overhead is such that we have recently

been forced to require a small reading fee. (Usually somewhere between seventy-five and five hundred dollars.) Naturally the fee will be deducted from our commission upon publication."

"Please enclose payment with your manuscript and we will reply to you immediately upon completion of the reading." They always end with, "We look forward to hearing from you soon."

The novice writer manages to scrape up the money, write out the check, (but not always in that order), and send it with the manuscript. Six months later, he or she finds a large, wrinkled package in the mailbox. Inside is the manuscript with a sticky-note attached. The note is flowery, courteous, and polite. It always starts with, "Sorry for the delay."

In so many words it says, "The manuscript sucks."

The novice is left with the knowledge that he or she has just paid someone to insult his or her (or both if he or she happens to be a Wurlitzer) life's work.

Once in a blue moon (typically the third October 18th of every odd leap year) an agent actually accepts a new writer's manuscript. Sort of. In this case the sticky-note is replaced with a full size page. Hidden among all the flowery verbiage is the statement, "Your work might be publishable if . . ."

The agent will then proceed to ask that the first half of the work be rewritten and the second half replaced. To be returned, of course, for further evaluation, with another reading fee enclosed. This represents the first go 'round of a repeating cycle that allows the agent familiarization with the writer's style, level of commitment, and depth of checking account.

There has been much heated debate regarding the attachment of reading fees. It is the writers themselves who are doing most of the yelling. Many are appalled at the concept, the mere thought of paying to have their manuscripts read and critiqued.

Closer inspection shows that the majority of those affronted are already-published, established authors who have to keep a bulldozer in the garage to plow the hordes of agents from their driveways every morning.

Depending on the type of work you are doing and your own marketing skills, knowledge and perseverance, an agent may not be necessary. If you are writing an article on the eradication of mealy bugs from okra stems, your markets will be a bit limited. The smaller your potential markets, the easier they are to locate and contact. Hence, an agent's services may not be required.

Say you have just completed a 1500 page manuscript commemorating the hardships suffered by your great aunt in raising three kids. Say one kid is in an Ohio prison, one is living on welfare in Idaho, and the last is hitchhiking his way to Australia. The obvious high reader appeal (?) and wide potential market (??), not to mention movie and sequel right possibilities (???), easily indicate that it may be best to get some help.

Lists of agents are printed in other how-to-write-a-book books (which cost much more than this one). You can, of course, look in the Yellow Pages of such publishing centers as New York, Chicago, Omaha, and Cooter Creek.

Do not send your manuscript to an agent without first getting permission to do so. If you ignore this advise and send it anyway, you will get it back, if you are lucky. If you are very lucky, you will get a brief but humiliating letter with it. Unless you have an ego of granite, play by the rules. Always enclose a return, stamped envelope. Pre-printed rejection cards may also help to ingratiate you with agents and publishers, and your wording may be kinder.

Most agents do not have any desire to help you sell your work until you are famous enough to no longer need their services. Try, therefore, to choose an agent who specializes in books similar to the one you are working on. Establish a dialogue. Do this after your book is fairly well developed but before it is complete. Somewhere in this time frame you should be able to demonstrate to the agent the direction it is taking as well as your skills as a writer. A good agent can and will advise you as to the things that do and do not sell.

Establishing dialogue with a good agent is really very simple. All you have to do is pay cash and beg the agent repeatedly to read your work. After the cash has come to rest in the agent's bank account you will receive word, in the form of a brief but humiliating letter. It will say whether the agent will even consider representing you and if so, what changes to your work or other requirements will be necessary to open the door. Very large numbers followed by "%" will also be included.

Please keep in mind that the agent is far too busy to actually read your manuscript him/herself. If you are accepted, however, he/she will engage the services of an intelligent high school student, college freshman, or out of work professional critic to read your manuscript and report back as to its genuine merits, at a good bit less than minimum wage, of course.

Once you have secured an agent's assistance, be certain that you have a written agreement specifying the agent's responsibilities, compensation, and the length of your relationship. Have it reviewed by your attorney, who will charge a percentage fee based on the following formula: 100% - agent's commission = attorney fee. Locating and securing an agent's services may sound frustrating, humiliating, and expensive. Good job! You're with the program.

Remember, once you have succeeded, a good agent can save you much frustration, humiliation, and expense with the publisher's editor. The choice to hire an agent is both difficult and personal. The publishing industry releases figures from time to time to assist the beginning writer in making this choice.

Of the tens of thousands of writers trying to publish first novels, approximately two hundred fifty of them succeeded in 1990.

In industry vernacular, this is known as a Gotcha.

Part II (Roman for Part 2)
PUBLISHER'S EDITORS

These are the important people. Editors work for the publishing companies. They are the ones who decide which manuscripts will be turned into books. They are also the ones who spend hours upon countless hours reading all the really dumb stuff sent to them by all those other people who think they can write. Editors work much harder than agents. They have a lot more responsibility. They may also charge smaller reading fees.

Go figure.

Beginning writers normally send their first completed, toiled-over manuscripts to editors, not by name, just "Editor". They also normally tell how great they are or will soon become, how they got their idea for Their Book, how much money they will settle for (typically $10,000, minimum), and what a good deal it will be for the publishing company if and when their Great American Novel is put into print.

These packages usually get thrown into a thing called a slush pile.

Mistakenly thought by neophytes as a semi-organized file of sorts, it is actually a dank corner where editors and their fellow employees keep their wet soggy boots in the winter and their sweaty handball clothing all year round.

Manuscripts that arrive in this manner are known in the trade as 'over the transom' manuscripts. The phrase is no doubt derived from the fact that some editors have been caught trying to dispose of them by throwing them out the window. One would think it obvious in a twenty story office building, but some folks get desperate. One can always tell which window belongs to an editor. It is the one with the dumpsters beneath and down wind a bit from it.

A seasoned writer usually contacts an editor with a thing called a precis. (pree-sis.) Seasoned writers are on the right track here because they get an advance (**money**) for their books without having to write the whole darned thing.

A precis can be thought of as a five-part package.

Part One is the query letter. It introduces the author telling how great he/she is, how he/she got his/her idea for The Book, and what a great deal it will be for the publishing company, and so forth.

Part Two is an outline. A list of the chapters, chapter titles, and proposed length of the work.

Part Three is an annotated outline. It is a list of the chapters, with titles and length, and a paragraph or two describing what's happening in each chapter.

Part Four consists of one or two finished chapters of The Book.

Part five is an SSAE. Not to be confused with a Self Starting Automobile Engine (It wouldn't fit in the mail anyway.), an SSAE is defined as a Stamped, Self-Addressed Envelope. This supposedly is so that the editor can return the precis if it isn't suitable according to the publisher's needs, moral code, marketing timetable, digestive track serenity, personal preferences, and pocketbook.

Be sure to put double the postage required on the envelope, because by the time the manuscript is returned, the Post Office will have raised the rates.

Notice that seasoned writers never mention payment. Asking for money is Not Smart. It may be difficult to understand why editors would pay more attention to an unfinished, outlined work rather than a finished one, but that's the way it goes. Frankly we don't understand it either.

The odds that either a manuscript or precis will be accepted by an editor are somewhere in the area of 100,000 to one. The one that is accepted will show up in the mail in the original package, returned with an added letter (instead of a two or three line mimeographed eight-and-one-half by one inch strip of paper) similar to that as mentioned in the Agent section above.

The editor will typically proceed to ask that the first half of the work be replaced and the second half rewritten, which is just the opposite of the agent's request. The editor's request is stated in a manner that carries a well hidden hint, "You no rewrite, me no publish."

Because editors are somewhat more realistic as compared to agents, they do not all look for the next book market superstar. Well, okay. They look for it, sure. They just don't expect it of every single thing they publish. Even though YOU certainly won't have to concern yourself with them, you might be curious about those volumes that do not manage to reach the bestseller lists.

There are two categories or levels of fiction below bestseller. They are called Middies and Shredders.

Middies are those books that sell well enough so the publisher, editor, agent, attorney, and (if it can't be avoided) author get paid. Contrary to popular opinion, these are the works that keep the business of publishing rolling, the industry's pop and pizza so to speak. These usually prove to be a great disappointment to all concerned, mainly because they are not bestsellers.

Shredders are those books that were printed in great quantities, heavily promoted by big-budget marketing firms, big-name public personalities, and advertised to the hilt. For reasons that escape everybody, they didn't sell at volumes even resembling those either the publishers or marketeers had guessed. Instead, some cheapy book exposing the secret daydreams of Princess Di as written by the woman who pinned her gown during a fitting sells millions. The remaining volumes, sitting in the great warehouses of the publishers, are shredded to be repackaged into blown-in insulation for homes and offices or paper mache kits for resale to Cub Scout troops.

There is very little concern about books categorized as shredders. This is because once the decision has been made, no one — editor, publisher, agent, or even author — seems to bear any recollection of the book's existence.

As we stated earlier, editors are more reasonable people. Their main concern is with grammar, spelling, story line, punctuation, and whether the work contains enough sex, terror, bloodshed, and insanity to appeal to the general public. The concern with grammar, however, is slightly diminished in those cases where the book is intended for children.

HERE'S HOW TO BEAT IT.

In choosing a publisher, be sure the work that the publisher publishes meets your standards for content, quality, and marketing. Your public library will have a number of large volumes of reference books where, in a few hours, you might be able to locate one. Or look between Psychologists and Quilts in the yellow pages.

Once you have located such a firm, gain access to a window ledge just outside the chief editor's office. Take with you a cage full of pigeons and live there for a couple of weeks, until the pigeons learn that the perch is "home".

The third week, from a nearby yet hidden location, every morning fasten a firecracker to the left leg and a few pages of your work to the right leg of one of the pigeons. Light the firecracker and release the bird.

It may take a week or two, but you will get a reaction. This is the only sure-fire method we are aware of to get an editor's attention.

If this method doesn't appeal to you, (afraid of heights, love pigeons, etc.) you are certainly free to send money to the publisher as a bribe. In a few days you will receive your work by return mail. The cash will have been replaced with a brief but humiliating letter leaving you free to choose another publisher and start over.

Part III (Roman for Part 3)
PUBLICATION

Within weeks of the writer's threat to use his computer as a footstool, vault his typewriter through the editor's bedroom window, commit suicide, or insert his/her/its manuscript into anatomical history, the other people involved get together over Jack Daniels tea to discuss the writer's future.

If it is decided that the writer has paid his dues (read allowed himself to be treated rudely enough long enough) the work is okayed for publication. The publisher will contact the writer, or his next of kin, to inform her/him/it that he is satisfied with the work.

The accepted manuscript is usually returned to the author covered with a multitude of multicolored markings resembling the hieroglyphics of a long-extinct civilization. It is the writer's responsibility to initially decipher the scribbles before trying to learn just what to do about it. Upon receipt of yet another rewritten copy, the editor will now send it to another department to have it typeset, in preparation for printing.

The author will then be sent something called galleys. By this method the author is given his last chance to review the work to give it his final blessing and to be sure that the editor and typesetter didn't flub it up.

Checks and balances? Sort of.

Somewhere in the neighborhood of one-and-a-half to five years after the writer has sent in his manuscript, the book goes to print. That is, of course, assuming that all has gone smoothly thus far. After this stage, things really go to hell.

Part IV (Roman for Part 4)
CRITICS

Research by the authors has shown that critics come in two basic types.

Type A critics; witty, incisive, intelligent, down-to-earth, brave, clean, and reverent.

Type B critics; low-down, mean-spirited, shallow, cowardly but brutal, and callous.

How do you tell the difference? How can one be certain that only a Type A critic will review one's book? Can critics make or break your book? The answers to these questions are, well, critical. We will share our knowledge in this area with you via the following exchange of letters. Incidentally, these letters were unsolicited. (In fact, we didn't even want them.)

Dear Adam and Darv,

How can I tell a Type A critic from a Type B? I need your answer because I'm writing a term paper for Miss Jorgensen's 11th grade English class.

Please hurry. It's due next week Tuesday.

Your Friend, Bobby

Dear Bobby,

What a coincidence! Adam and I knew Miss Jorgensen in college! She was a hot little number back then, we can tell you. Whooeee!!

We will be delighted to answer your question, and in time for your paper, too.

Please send $50.00 cash.

Your Friends, Darv & Adam

Dear Darv and Adam,

You cheesedips!!! Here's your $50.00. Hurry! I'm desperate! There will be another $50.00 in it for you if you can send me some good "Miss Jorgensen" stories.

Your acquaintance, Bobby

Dear Bobby,

Thanks for the fifty bucks. We have done volumes of research concerning the answer to your question. Here it is.

    1. Write something.
        A. Write it well.
        B. Pour your heart, soul, and guts into it.
    2. Have it published. (As if you really could, you sniveling little creep!)
    3. Read any reviews that may follow.
        A. If you like them, the critic is Type A.
        B. If you don't, he's a Type B.

Sincerely, Adam & Darv

P.S. Meet us by the teeter-totter at midnight. Bring small, unmarked bills. Our stories will curl your toes!

Dear Mssrs. Harfield and Poszar,

It was nice to hear that you had inquired about me of one of my students. I remember you both from college days. Oh, do I!

Bobby, one of my students, has requested that I ask you how one can be certain that only Type A critics will review one's book. Bobby said something about having to pay you for the answers. Ridiculous, I know, but he seems convinced.

Ah, the bygone days of college. How well do I remember. I still remember what you did to

107

Daddy's Cadillac the night of the Big Game.

I also remember that you still owe him several thousand dollars for it. Now that I know where you are, I'm sure you will give Bobby his answers free of charge.

Right, Peeky and Geeky?

Retrospectively Yours,

Stella Jorgensen

Stella Baby!

What a surprise it was to get a letter from you! You sure haven't lost your sense of humor, have you. Ha Ha Ha! Think of it. All those years of college and you're still in the 11th grade! Just kidding. Ha Ha Ha!

But seriously. We do vaguely recall corresponding with a certain Bobby person. The only way we can remember his note is because, for some reason unknown to either of us, he put a handful of Monopoly money into the letter. How is he?

When you see him again, please ask about his health. Ask him how his knees are.

Titillatingly Yours, Adam and Darv

P.S. Did you ever get that cute little tattoo removed?

Darv and Adam,

You jerks! Here is the real money - not that you earned it. Boy was Miss Jorgensen upset! She said that the story you told about her wasn't true, and that she'd never even SEEN a topless Mother Goose costume. She did want me to pass a message to you, though.

She wanted me to ask if you remember Bruno. They just got engaged. I met this Bruno guy when I showed her your first letter.

Wow! They sure grew them big back in your day! How did he get that number tattooed on

108

his forehead, anyway?

More importantly, can a critic really make or break a book?

Your friend, Bobby

Dear Mr. Bobby,

Yes, a critic can make or break a book, but only if he writes for 'People' magazine. Nobody reads those eggheads that review books in literary magazines, and a bad review in a mag like 'Time' can only help sales.

It has certainly been a pleasure to correspond with such a fine young man as yourself. Enclosed please find $150.00 cash. Bruno suggested we send it along. You really took our little joke seriously, didn't you? Ha Ha Ha!

Best of luck to you in what will obviously be a fine and affluent future.

Please give our kindest regards to your Miss Jorgensen, what an excellent teacher she must be.

Worshipfully, Adam and Darv

P.S. If you happen to see Mr. Bruno, please inform him that we have moved and will send him our new address "real soon".

Part V (Roman for Part 5)
VANITY PRESSES

Consider this. You submit your work to fifteen agents and/or publishers along with a reading fee of $250.00 to each. That's $3,750.00! If you are very fortunate, the tenth one agrees to publish your book. A couple of hundred strangers buy it before the remaining 4800 copies go to the shredder. From then on, nobody in the industry will ever talk to you again.

Now, consider this. You give the manuscript and $3,500.00 to a short, fat, swarthy man who has ink stains on his hands and an office in a mobile home. He is a publisher working in the dark recesses of the industry known as a vanity press. He promises to promote the book for you so that you can sell the paperback and movie rights for millions of dollars. He even runs off a hundred or so copies (which, by the way, you can autograph in less than an hour). Your book has been interestingly bound in a mud-brown cover, with title canted at an interesting angle to the pages. He promotes your book diligently for a couple of minutes, selling 99 copies to your relatives.

You have saved $250.00, hundreds of hours of rewriting, months of waiting for rejection slips, the agony of writers' cramp, and the problems locating an attorney to develop an estate plan capable of disposing of millions of dollars before the government can get its grimy, bureaucratic hands on it. And all your relatives now have documented proof as to the sort of genuinely brilliant sort of person you finally turned out to be.

In addition, while you were saving all this time you were working at a real job where somebody was paying you BY THE HOUR for your labor. Think of it! What a great way to live! "Wage" and "Salary" are beautiful words compared to "Potential Royalties".

Part VI (Roman for Part 6)
PERIODICALS

Maybe you have chosen newspapers or magazines as your stairway to the top, as Darv has done. You may sell your articles or column directly to various papers or magazines, or to a company that sells syndicated columns to many newspapers. Each method is equally futile.

The adversity will, however, greatly develop your character.

Part VII (Roman for Part 7)
SPECIAL NOTES

All the activities mentioned in this book, Creation, Writing, Rewriting, Editing, More Rewriting, Agenting, Additional Rewriting, Publisher's Editors, and Even More Rewriting may take anywhere from a month to two years each. All this struggling and fussing is what is known as "paying one's dues."

It is thought to be that which gives a writer depth, focus, and maturity through contact with the reality of the business. The typical net effect is one of sleepless nights, unpaid bills, and ulcers. It is best to begin your writing career when you are Very Young. It is also best to come to an early awareness that in truth you do not choose a publisher, nor does a publisher choose you. If and when the two of you actually do come together, it will be because of blind luck, otherwise known as Divine Intervention.

Part VIII (Roman for Part 8)
PARTING COMMENTS

Many -if not most- agents refuse to represent a writer who has not authored at least two books which have already been published.

Many -if not most- editors refuse to work with a writer who is without the representation of an agent.

Go figure.

13
MARKETING

There are strangers out there whose job is something called marketing. They are called marketeers and no, they probably do not wear beanies with big ears on them, at least not on a regular basis. And there are more than three in number. Male marketeers are usually named Bernie, females Gloria. Everyone a marketeer talks to is named Sweetheart.

In an effort to learn what marketing is from the source, we sent letters to a number of them. We introduced ourselves and explained that we were writing a book in which a relatively accurate and timely description of their chosen profession, especially as it pertains to bookselling, would be necessary. We also enclosed a questionnaire we felt would generate even more information.

Nobody replied.

Actually that is not entirely true. We did receive one of our own letters via return post. Something about postage due. We are on a budget.

In spite of this minor mishap, we decided to press on, as the British say. Therefore the next few paragraphs were written as though we had performed an actual face to face interview with a marketeer. We really did try to call one but the listing in our phone book jumped from Marble-Natural to Marriage- Family, Child & Individual Counselors.

"Good evening."
"Good evening."
"And you are."
"Igor Lobrau."
"Well, Mr. Lobrau, thank you for allowing us to talk with you."
"You're welcome. Do I really get a year's subscription to Playtoy magazine for this?"
"We'll discuss it after the interview, Mr. Lobrau. Now, you are a marketeer by profession. Is that right?"
"Yeah, I'm a marketeer."
"And how did you come to be one?"
"Layoff."
"Pardon me?"
"The county laid off all its pullers."
"Pullers?"
"You know, the people who pull weeds around the signs along the highway."
"I see."
"Well, it was January."
"That's unfortunate."
"Not really, my knees were starting to bother me anyway. And the Army requires a high school diploma."
(Pause)
"Would you be kind enough to define marketing for us?"
"Sure."
"Would you be kind enough to define marketing for us today please, Mr. Lobrau?"
"About that subscription . . ."
"About that definition . . ."
"Okay, okay. Marketing can be defined as the discovery and use of methods whereby a widespread yet focused subgroup of society is persuaded to make a monetary decision in the purchasing mode. As it pertains to the

114

bookselling industry, this subgroup could be approximated to be those individuals who purchase books. A sub-subgroup, if you will, could be those individuals who buy books and who can also read. In fact, this is the very sub-sub that has gotten virtually all of the marketing focus and funding in the recent past. Quite unfair in my personal estimation, yet it is deemed unwise to perform contradictorily to the economic mainstream flow. Don't buck the bucks as we say around the office, don't you know. How'd I do?"

"Would you be kind enough to translate that for our readers?"

"Sure."

"Into English?"

"Just between us?"

"Just between us."

"Promise you won't print it?"

"My editor at Playtoy won't be very happy . . ."

"Right. Well, it's coming up with -and using- whatever it takes to persuade, cajole, con or trick people who really aren't interested into buying something that they can't afford, preferably on credit. Here's how it works.

"The author is paid $.75 for every book sold. (Of this, his agent, if he has one, what with reading fees and commissions and such, gets an average of $.74 to $13.75 per book of this money.)

"The editor gains around $.50 per book.

"The publishing company receives about $1.50 each.

"Materials; paper, ink, glue, etc. cost approximately $1.20 per book. The finished book is sold to retail outlets for $12.50 and hits the shelves at $19.95 a copy, the remainder being explained away as advertising expense.

"It is then discounted to $17.50 for sale through order-by-mail catalogs, with $4.75 added for postage and handling, which, in fact, cost about a buck. Simple, isn't it?"

"Thank you, Mr. Lobrau."

"Hey what about my Playtoy subscription?"

"We'll see that you get it. Do you have nineteen ninety-five?"

"For what?"

"Your subscription. We didn't say it was free."

The author occasionally plays a part in marketing. When he/she does, it consists of first selling books to his/her family members and, second, traveling from bookstore to bookstore, city to city, and country to country to sign copies of his/her book for all the new customers. This is called a promotional tour. Some publishers will occasionally offer to pay the author's traveling expenses.

Should this happen to you, the first thing to do is to go to the mall. Purchase the best running shoes you can afford and a large suitcase. You'll need it to haul all the bus tickets in.

THE PUBLIC

In general terms, the book buying public has been described as educated, informed, of middle to upper-middle income, having somewhat more than average free time, and possessing preferences that can change from poetry to anthologies of the author's kindergarten training toCivil War love affairs to twenty-fifth century outer space genocide in the span of a couple of weeks.

During our research, (okay, during our phone call) nine out of ten publishing firm spokespersons (okay, Gloria) typified the public with a specific yet common term.

Assuming this to be part of the industry jargon, buzzword-wise, and given the impressions we received during our numerous interviews, we can only guess that this stands for:

Tasteless Ugly Rubes Kicking Editors & You (authors) Sadistically.

In fact, the biggest headache of the majority of publishers is in trying to predict what THE PUBLIC will be interested in reading next year. (Naturally, those who publish Romances and Westerns don't have to be concerned with this. They merely put new titles on old works and republish them. They learned this "marketing masterstroke" from composer/singer Neil Diamond).

116

For our purposes, the public is defined as anyone who buys books. No, we dussn't give a holler or a hoot iff'n thay kin reed er nott.

Beating this system is a for-sure Zen, do-it-in-your-sleep, transcendental project. Here are two ideas, which we have labeled A and B for easy reference, proving our creative abilities.

A. A lot of people are really busy. They don't want to spend a lot of time wandering around bookstores learning what book is the immediate ultimate. Instead, they pick up their daily paper and read the book review. And then they base their book purchases on them! Imagine that!

So what you, the up-and-coming writer do is take out an ad in the newspaper. Write it so that it looks exactly like it was done by one of those critic types that we have described elsewhere in this book. We know it will be difficult trying to imitate some frustrated literary hack who is probably newly (for the fourth time) divorced due to a severe alcohol problem, has bad breath, and a naturally cranky disposition.

Give it your best shot, though. The rewards are great. You have two ways to go from this point. You can:

1.) Write a syrupy, glowing review referring to yourself as the next Shakespeare, Hemingway, King, or Irving.

2.) Create a country Sunday morning fire-and-brimstone review that recommends the book be saved for emergencies (to be used to start fires in the event of a nuclear winter) and being sure to make severe personal accusations concerning the sanity, sexual preferences, and planet of origin as regards the author (you).

Here's how to choose which review to use. If you already have a completed manuscript use review 1.). If not, use 2.). The nastier the review, the less time the public will spend skimming through your book before carrying it to the checkout line.

If you are unable to write one of these reviews due to religious principles, go to your local library and copy one, changing the names and a few words here and there.

Once you have run your ad, clip out copies from the papers in all the coffee shops, dentist office waiting rooms, barber shops, and libraries in town. Or, if you're in a pinch, buy a bunch of papers. When clipping, remember to carefully trim off the word "advertisement".

If you already have a manuscript, send it and review 1.) to a publisher, calling your advertisement review a "professional reference." If you don't, just send review 2.).

Get your family or friends to start rumors, always referring to you by your most bizarre name. (If for instance your name is John Yance Jones, the rumors should be phrased, "Did you see the latest Yance novel? Outrageous!" It is also helpful if they mention that the book is loaded with sex and violence, and that most of the characters are based on local townspeople.

Have postcards printed announcing your book and send one to every fourth person in your phone book. Turn down all party invitations, muttering something about having to "do" Donahue. Soon your phone will ring.
"Hello?" you will say.
"Sweetheart! This is Bernie. Let's do lunch."

B. Publish it yourself! We realize this may require that you write or at least copy something to serve as your novel but, hey, no plan is perfect. Run off at least three hundred copies.

How? Your employer's copy machine is an excellent candidate. Don't be concerned with the supplies you may consume. Running out of copier supplies is a capital offense in the majority of offices, second only to purchasing the wrong coffee machine filters. In other words, it is typically overstocked. A case or two of copy paper and a dozen toner cartridges will never be missed.

Don't worry if the machine breaks down. Most office copy machines do on a regular basis anyway. Most firms purchase maintenance contracts. That's where your employer pays a regular fee that covers any and all required copy machine repairs. In other words, they'll never know.

Be sure to plan ahead. Run your copies when the bosses are out to lunch, preferably on a Friday. That will give you, on average, at least three hours.

Once you have your copies, trim them so that they will fit into video cassette boxes. Most offices have the perfect tool for this, too. It looks like the thing sold between three and four AM on Channel 29 to dice potatoes, slice carrots, and peel recalcitrant rutabagas.

Package your book in video cassette boxes. Buy or make three different styles of labels, each one cleverly disguising the title within the graphics. (See our next book, '1001 More Creative Uses For Office Machinery') Your first label will resemble a video on hunting and fishing.

"Sportsmen" videos are consumed like candy by men who can't read without moving their lips. They will be so embarrassed when they get home and discover that they have actually purchased a book that they will dupe their friends into buying one also.

The second label should appear to tout an exercise video. Women over thirty buy these at a rate of about one a week. And, if the picture on the label is racy enough, their husbands will buy them a copy whether they want it or not.

The third label should be covered with cartoon figures and the letter "G" in large bold type. If you can interest the kids, their parents will have no choice.

14
HUMOR

We have chosen to paraphrase a famous statement regarding humor.

You can fool all the people some of the time.
And you can fool some of the people all of the time.
Especially if you're a Presidential candidate.

Or something like that.

What we're trying to tell you is that there are some folks who just won't get a chuckle out of your work no matter what you do, or how outrageously you do it. So why bother?

As you have easily seen from the example we have set in the seriousness of this book, we feel that there is no room in either fiction or nonfiction for silliness, baloney, bilge, bosh, bull, bunk, drivel, fiddlesticks, foolishness, frivolity, junk, malarkey, nonsense, poppycock, rot, rubbish, schlock, or trivia.

Unless, of course, your name happens to be Danny Kaye, Red Skelton, Red Buttons, ReddFox, Richard Pryor, Tom or Dick Smothers, Tom Bodett, Carol Burnett, Jerry Lewis, Dean Martin, Steve Martin, Martin Short, Milton Berle, George Jessel, Shari

Lewis, Paul Winchell, Rich Little, Joe Piscopo, Victor Borge, Morey Amsterdam, Sid Caesar, Peter Sellers, Will Rogers, W. C. Fields, Spike Jones, Jay Leno, Jim Varney, Bob Newhart, Jackie Gleason, Wayne, Garth, Charlie Chaplin, Mel Brooks, Whoopie Goldberg, Alan King, Eddie Murphy, Jonathan Winters, John Candy, John Biner, John Belushi, Jim Belushi, Fred Flintstone, Danny DeVito, Tom Hanks, Gallagher, Bob Hope, Dave Barry, Buddy Hackett, Yakov Smirnoff, Abbot or Costello, Garrison Keillor, Shelley Berman, Shelley DuVal, Groucho, Harpo, or Whats-his-name Marks, Rosy O' Donnel, Rosanne Barr, Douglas Adams, Rob Reiner, Art Buchwald, Andy Rooney, Mickey Rooney, Chevy Chase, Lilly Tomlin, Neil Gaiman, Terry Pratchett, Winston Groom, Robert Fulghum, Douglas W. Clark, Jack Benny, Ernie Kovaks, Howie Mandel, Howdy Doody, Bozo, Tim Conway, Bernadette Peters, Pee Wee Herman, Popeye, Robin Williams, Stan Laurel, Olliver Hardy, Arnold Schwarzzenegger, Dick VanDyke, Joan Rivers, Bill Cosby, Phil Silvers, George Burns, Gracy Allen, Benny Hill, Danny Thomas, Larry, Moe, Curly, Joe, Shemp, or the guy who played the villain in Blazing Saddles. And of course if you happen to be a member of the United States Congress.

Yes, silliness, baloney, bilge, bosh, bull, bunk, drivel, fiddlesticks, foolishness, frivolity, junk, malarkey, nonsense, poppycock, rot, rubbish, schlock, and trivia may have their devotees, but this represents such a minute segment of society that attempting to sell a book to such would amount to little more than an exercise in silliness, baloney, bilge, bosh, bull, bunk, drivel, fiddlesticks, foolishness, frivolity, junk, malarkey, nonsense, poppycock, rot, rubbish, schlock, and trivia.

In truth, the only reason that we gave the topic of humor its own chapter was to show you how full of silliness, baloney, bilge, bosh, bull, bunk, drivel, fiddlesticks, foolishness, frivolity, junk, malarkey, nonsense, poppycock, rot, rubbish, schlock, and trivia the concept is.

15
MISCELLANIA

No, this chapter is not about the travels of a very popular Lania nor an industrialized city-state dedicated to ballistic ordnance.

It's the happy home of all the profundity we couldn't manage to put elsewhere.

A. Length
Determining the length of your book can be agonizing, especially if you actually intend to plan the thing prior to writing it. Too long, and who (other than bricklayers) will want it. Too short and you risk being forced into adding wide margins, lots of graphs and pictures, a foreword, a prelude, preface, introduction, triple spacing, an index, a bibliography, an appendix, a couple of blank pages at each end, and a whole lot of other stuff that will drive the cost of the book up.

Our advice is don't worry about it, just write the darned thing. If you then submit it to eighty-six publishers, forty-three will require you to add material. The other forty-three will insist that you abridge. The eighty-seventh publisher will break the tie. Moral: please yourself.

B. Voice
Choosing a voice to use in your book is probably the second decision you will make, right after answering the question most asked

of writers (usually by an abrasive boor, with a whiny, wheedling voice), "What's it about?" This second decision, the Choice of Voice, is capitalized not because it is so dag gummed important, but because it makes such a nifty little rhyme.

Second person, third person, first; which will it be? Second person, third person, first; doesn't really matter to me!

"John scratched his head."

"Mildred watched John scratch his head."

"Hi, I'm John. Excuse me but my head itches."

Or, if you are feeling adventurous, try the pluperfect fourth voice of the next tense.

"Mildred gaped in amazement at the others having had considered John pondering his formerly upcoming and really compelling bout of head scratching."

You may be more familiar with the idiomatic name for this voice used by English grammar teachers everywhere, except in non-English speaking parts of the world (where they have no English grammar teachers). They call it the "what-the-hey?" voice.

C. Commitment
In order to become rich and famous through one's writing, indeed to achieve a level wherein one can live above the Federal Minimum Poverty Level, a certain amount of commitment is required. (Please note: It is illegal to feel poor unless you meet this standard.) By this we do not mean spending a fixed number of weeks or months in a monastery atop a Tibetan peak. It might help, but it is not the main topic discussed here. Commitment may best be thought of as an investment in your future.

This investment is comprised of three parts, best remembered as The Three P's: Practice, Personal sacrifice, and Pself discipline.

1. Practice.

Practice can best be thought of as the middle finger of commitment. You must practice! Practice spelling. Practice punctuation.?! Practice dialogue. Practice developing characters, plots and subplots, and weaving them all together. Practice baring your very soul to the big white page or the little green screen. Practice staying awake. Practice counting your toes.

2. Personal Sacrifice.

The liquid that keeps this writers' enema flowing is the conscious realization that in order to achieve one's aims, one must face certain amounts of personal sacrifice. If you are team-writing, in order to achieve the aims of two, both must face it.

According to a recent poll (Adam asked Darv, Darv asked Adam) the following are acceptable and may be considered red badges of courage.

Skip the next episode of Night Court.
Tell your spouse that you'll come to bed in just a minute.
Skip the next two episodes of Cheers.
Delay changing the water in the fish tank.
Hold off on having that flat tire fixed. Where can you go anyway, on what you're earning as a writer?
Skip your turn at bathing the kids.
Wait a couple of weeks after your spouse has determined that you should call an exterminator.
Let the bills slide another week or two.
Paper the kitchen-next year.
Ask to be excused when the in-laws visit.
Ask to be excused when your family visits.
Don't ask to be excused if you break wind.
Save time by seeing how far the family car will travel with the fuel gage on "E".
Charge your writing supplies on your VISA card.
Charge your writing supplies on your spouse's VISA card.
Lavish gifts on your agent.
Lavish bigger gifts on your editor.

Treat both your agent and editor to evenings on the town with paid escorts and massages, and charge it to your spouse's VISA card.

3. Pself Discipline.

Self-discipline comes in many forms. The idea is to achieve the "Writer's Mindset" and stick to it like a wet tongue on a sled runner at ten below zero. Some people feel that disciplined writers must either write a minimum number of pages or for a minimum amount of time every day.

In our opinion there are better litmuses than a pile of pages or the buzzing of a clock's alarm. A truly disciplined writer will:

Write through the Superbowl.
Miss meals.
Continue in spite of the leaking roof, plugged drains, peeling paint, and warping floor.
Forget to feed the dog.
Forget to feed the kids.
Continue to pound at the keyboard through power outages.
Fail to notice that the dog starved to death four months ago.
Not realize that the kids have married and moved away.
Ignore the fact that his/her toenails are now longer than his/her toes.
Surpass the Yogis of the Far East in bladder and bowel control.

D. Setting

For years the great impressionist Claude Monet (no, he did not do John Wayne, Ed Sullivan, or Richard Nixon) dashed all over France and England to paint landscapes. In his later years, he settled down on his sumptuous Giverny garden (known in the United States as a swamp) to paint water lilies.

He painted big water lilies, little water lilies, green water lilies, and yellow water lilies. He painted them in morning light, evening light, summer light, spring light, autumn light, in the rain and the sunlight.

"Bonjour, Claude," his wife would say every morning. "What would you like to do today, mon cher?"

"Ah, my little buttercup, I think I will go down by the pond and paint water lilies."

At that, Madame Monet would roll her eyes and ask herself why her husband couldn't be more like Degas and kick out an occasional sculpture of a horse or ballet dancer.

Likewise the setting of a book, the time(s) and place(s) in which the story takes place, can be macroscopic or microscopic. Each has its own rewards and challenges.

Readers of Sherlock Holmes mysteries can almost feel the freedom Doyle must have experienced when he would occasionally cut the great detective and Doctor Watson loose from the bonds of the apartment in which they existed.

Here we cannot resist introducing a new word meaning a rented abode one or more flights above ground level— upartment.

First of all, Holmes had to share the place with Watson, who must have been a terrible bore. Second, the place was cluttered with the collections common to Holmes' curious mind. Third, that incessant Jack Benny music played whenever Sherlock endeavored to formulate a solution. Finally, it reeked of pipe smoke and opium. Every now and again, however, Doyle settled Sherlock into the seat of a carriage rollicking through the foggy streets of a London evening, cobbles and all, the comforting bulge of a pistol in the pocket of his greatcoat.

If you have ever visited Universal Studios in Los Angeles, the little tram turning the corner of "Wall Street" carried you into the dusty western town where America has seen dozens of hombres bite the dust at high noon. And you probably groaned, "Oh, no. Not this damned town again!" Likewise when one picks up a "parlor mystery" the reaction might be, "Oh, no. Not this damned parlor again!"

Even if you are writing science fiction and can transport your characters on a subatomic level to any place or time at the push of a button, they still must have somewhere to go, and somewhere from which to leave. In other words, you must choose, and be able to express, settings. As confining as a particular setting may be, it can be equally difficult to open yourself to a grander scale.

Many of the great spy stories of the Seventies and Eighties flew from one exotic city to another, with an occasional mountaintop monastery used by Bulgarian terrorists thrown in for good measure. How difficult it must for the author to give the reader a feel for "place" while the characters rocket about the globe in such a manner. Kill a counterspy in Prague, get hit over the head by a beautiful Russian in Hong Kong, make love to an Italian in Hamburg, and steal military plans in Oak Ridge -all in the same day! It leaves one breathless.

The other component of setting, time, can be equally confining. For example, let's say you choose to write about 19th century Atlanta. You have just obligated yourself to hire an artist to paint a cover picture of a beautiful dark-haired belle with a long, flowing (and ripped) gown showing lots of thigh standing before a burning plantation as her scar-faced military lover crawls one-legged to her rescue from the background. You also bear the responsibility of knowing at least a little about the history, language and life of the era. You really shouldn't have your hero calling Jefferson Davis from the phone at the corner drugstore.

Writing in present time can be risky, too. We wonder what happened to the sales volume of the thousands of Cold War novels pitting CIA agents against the KGB after the Berlin Wall came tumbling down, not to mention the disassembly of the Soviet Union.

There are a number of useful tricks that can be employed if you are reluctant to stick yourself into one setting. First, you can label your book An Epic Saga of A Great American Family. This will let you roam the Old World back streets of Salerno in the 17th century, the casinos of Las Vegas in the 1990's, and the stinking hold of an 1845 slave ship all in the same volume. Second, you can use flashbacks.

Flashbacks are the Fly-Anywhere-United-Flies prepaid tickets of the literary world. Go anywhere, any time.

Third, opposite to flashbacks, you can utilize a vision of the future to carry your reader ahead in time and space. This is called foreshadowing or flash-forward, but who needs more fancy words to memorize?

Fourth, you can hire a New Age occult channeler as a consultant and do whatever you darned well please. People who read New Age literature don't care. They have all had get-a-grip-ectomies.

Your character is walking through a pasture when, suddenly, a very old man appears before her.
"I am Rakkama!" he thunders.
"Howdy, I'm Dorothy," Dorothy answers.
"I am an Egyptian Holy Man from the time of the Pharaohs. You must come with me. We will visit the Ghost of Christmas Past, who now rides with King Arthur and Prince Albert in a can."
"Okey dokey," says Dorothy as she is whisked up and away in a cloud of dust clutching a green crystal.

By the way, if you believe in New Age ideas, please send us $4,000.00. This is the correct price of this book in our next lives.

E. Team-Writing or Co-Authorship

Writing a book as a team makes about as much sense as playing tag-team doubles Ping-pong. A great game made foolish, and only so that more kids can use the table during lunch hour. The authors of this book collaborated only as the result of a chance meeting over a cup of coffee in an out-of-the-way cantina in southern

Michigan. Both happened to utter at the same moment, "I've half a mind to write a book."

We assure the reader that it will never happen again, the possible exception being a sequel to this one, and maybe twenty or thirty others. In truth, team writing can be great fun and fellowship. One of the authors of this book enjoyed the experience greatly. See Chapter Seventeen for more detail.

F. Technique

It has been said that there are as many techniques in creative writing as there are writers. It has also been said that each writer proclaims his as the optimum. It's true, these things have been said. But there is only one correct writing technique, ours.

Darv is a firm believer in developing a full outline prior to starting the actual writing. Each character is described on paper in his/her entirety. Short works would naturally require little more than a mental outline.

Adam is somewhat more spontaneous, sitting at the keyboard and letting the prose write itself. This is known as "making it up as you go along".

Does this sound like two very different techniques? Good job, you're still awake.

Keep in mind that the technique you find to be the most difficult is the best one for you. Writing should be fun, it should be natural and refreshing. Unfortunately, it's more often plain old hard work.

Since our discussion as to the Only Correct Technique did, we admit, get a little out of hand with one author smashing everything within reach and the other crying himself to sleep, we are offering a compromise technique as the Only.

It must be followed precisely.

Write the last chapter first.
Outline the first and second chapters.
Write the first chapter.
Outline the last and next-to-last.
Write the next-to-last chapter.
Outline the middle chapter.
Write the second and middle chapters.

Please note that if your work is more than five chapters this, the Only, is about as useful as a fan in a flood.

G. DRUGS

Many writers over the centuries have used certain chemical aids to get into the mood to write, or to stimulate their imaginations. Alcohol, caffeine, morphine, opium, and various other substances have played a large part in the careers of some writers. Short careers, on average.

Frankly, from a moral point of view we don't give a musk ox's belly rumble if you exist on hermetically grown Japanese heartnuts, berries and distilled water or pump your veins full of everything from used crankcase oil to year-old cabbage juice. Our opinion comes from a strictly practical point of view. Don't bother with chemicals, even if there happen to be other facets of your life besides writing.

For example, if you would like to also be a better spouse, parent, citizen, or human being, leave chemical "enhancers" alone. Besides, reality is so much more weird than fantasy that any kind of substance "aid" is completely unnecessary.

If you really want to get your writing into high gear, give yourself a large dose of reality. Here are a few examples. As of this writing:

Enough people have reported sighting a large sea ser-pent in Lake Erie that a telephone hotline has been opened in the Cleveland area.

A cat-scan machine has been built enabling the diagnosis of brain malfunctions in peoples' pets. "I think a scan is in order here, Mrs. Bargebase," says the veterinarian. "It may be a mild synaptic abnormality in the lower corticular zone. Surgery may be indicated, but we won't know until we get the results." "Oh my!" she exclaims. "Don't worry," the doctor reassures, "Even in the worst case scenario, prognosis for normal recovery is over 65% in guppies."

A bag of cocaine was found in a maintenance area at the space shuttle launch site.

Jim and Tammy Bakker are famous. Jim and Tammy Bakker were once rich.

Saddam Hussein was abused as a child.

The Mustang Ranch, one of this country's most famous brothels, has filed for bankruptcy due to tax problems. It was sold at auction. Until the sale, management was turned over to the US Government.

Bob Probert was "banned for life" from the National Hockey League for smuggling drugs. He was back on the ice the next year, playing for the Detroit Red Wings.

Texas is part of the United States.

The "Mainstream" Media still ignore Rush Limbaugh.

Reports of hypodermic needles found in cans of Pepsi are made in twenty-four states within the same week - all hoaxes.

Golf.

Consumer groups are demanding the recall of thousands of pickup trucks because their gas tanks explode when incendiary devices attached to them are detonated.

Weather experts have recorded the gradual lowering of average temperatures around the world. They are claiming the phenomenon is a result of global warming.

See what we mean?

H. Vulgarity

Is raw, steamy hot sex needed to sell books? Can you make your mark as a writer through extensive use of words that describe body parts, biological functions, and were coined with the sole intent of causing extreem hormonal imbalances, creating terror, or otherwise giving offense? Is mayhem, complete with blood-spurting stumps and wall-splattering intestines essential?

It depends.

It depends on the market or genre you wish to sell to. It also depends on how sound a sleeper you are. Some Western authors studiously avoid profanity to the point that its lack becomes ludicrous.

Picture if you will, two hide-tough, saddle-sore cowpokes. They have spent every evening for eight months squatting around campfires, spitting trail dust and passing bean gas. Having had nothing softer than a saddle between their knees, neither has seen a woman the full time. They finally ride into a bleak little Texas town and down a quart of Redeye. They get into an argument.

"Come on, you miserable side-winding yeller-bellied low down skunk! Take a swing!"
"You take one, you lame scorpion-eating sheep-loving lousy cook!"

Yeah right, you say, that's exactly how they would talk. They wouldn't dream of cussing. On the other hand, there is a very important rule of public speaking that is often extended to writing:

Never offend (and risk losing) a listener (or reader).

The fine point of this rule includes avoiding cussing, dirty jokes, and negative references to sex, race or religion. Audiences have been known to walk out. Readers can skip the dirty parts or throw the book away, unless it is one borrowed from the library. If you are the sort who actually enjoys this sort of thing, library books do have the advantage. They normally have deep smudges or dog-eared pages marking the sexy parts. And you don't have to hide them when you're finished, in fear of the children furthering their liberal educations.

So how do you resolve the dilemma? How does a writer maintain a sense of realism and not offend without sounding like a sap? We believe that you bought or borrowed this book to get answers, therefore we admit to the trust you have placed in us. We discussed this problem thoroughly. We discussed this problem loudly.

Frankly, we got into another genuine donnybrook over it. We swore at each other. We gouged one another in the eyes and bloodied each other's nose. We finally agreed to go home and sleep on it.

We ended up making passionate love to our wives instead. The answer will appear in our sequel.

I. PORNOGRAPHY

Sex sells, without a doubt. Some writers have attempted to shift their careers into high gear by creating pornography. We recommend against it for one primary reason.

Nobody manufactures pornographs any more!

134

17
TEAM WRITING: SOME CAUTIONS

In the event you choose to co-author a book with another person, be assured that regardless of the strength of your friendship going into the project, you will hate one another by the time you are done. Why? We offer some examples.

A. Editing one another's work.

"Darv, what do you mean, you changed paragraph ten? You jerk."

B. Differing styles.

"Adam, I absolutely adored your treatment of the topic of Agents. It was so-o-o-o precious, you dink."

C. Differing vocabulary.

The authors of this book spent more time discussing the word "dandle" than they spent writing the outline.

D. Communication.

Telephone calls are expensive.

E. Transmitting drafts.

The authors started mailing printed copies (hardcopies for hardbodies) back and forth for editing and re-writing. Finally, running out of paper and patience, computer disks were exchanged, along with the following notes.

"Darv—send a new copy of disks 2 and 4. Both were eaten by the post office."
"Adam—what do you mean, Chapter Seventeen got erased?"
"Darv—your fault, not mine."
"Adam—you should tell your mother that combat boots now come in designer colors."

All problems aside, we did enjoy cooperating on this book, even though we did have to make up an entirely new Chapter Seventeen, or face having to re-write the table of contents. Fortunately, we live over 100 miles apart, or we would have killed each other by now.

Saying that we enjoyed the project and discussing murder in the same paragraph may seem contradictory, but you must understand that both authors are working on mystery novels. Thus, contemplation of hands-on experience has been enjoyable, professionally speaking.

Yo Darv. That was Chapter Sixteen what got erased.
It was Chapter Seventeen, Adam.
So where is Chapter Sixteen, then smart guy? Hmm?
Ohmygod, we didn't do one!
Told ya!
Adam, are you sure that you're erasing these notes from the manuscript?
Sure thing, Boss!

APPENDIX

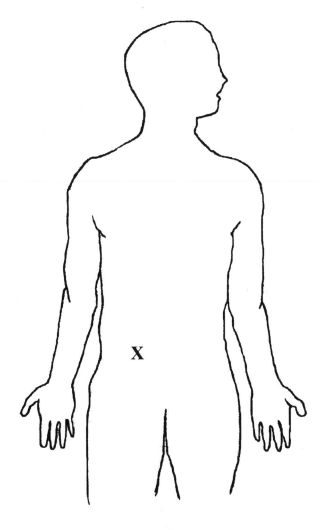

BIBLIOGRAPHY

Adams, Douglas. **The Hitchhiker's Guide To The Galaxy**. New York, NY, 1979.

Adams, Douglas. **Life, The Universe and Everything**. New York, NY, 1982.

Appelbaum, Judith. **How To Get Happily Published**. New York, NY, 1988.

Asimov, Janet and Isaac. **How To Enjoy Writing**. New York, NY, 1987.

Balkin, Richard. **A Writer's Guide to Book Publishing**. New York, NY, 1981.

Beckson, Karl. **Literary Terms: A Dictionary**. New York, NY, 1989.

Block, Lawrence. **Spider, Spin Me a Web: Lawrence Block on Writing Fiction**. Cincinnati, OH, 1988.

Block, Lawrence. **Writing the Novel: from Plot to Print**. Cincinnati, OH, 1987.

Bly, Robert W. **The Copywriter's Handbook**. New York, NY, 1990.

Book, Cassandra L. et al. **Human Communication: Principles, Contexts, and Skills**. New York, NY, 1980.

Brandreth, Gyles. **the Joy of Lex.** New York, NY, 1983.

Brown, Rita Mae. **Starting From Scratch**. New York, NY, 1988.

Burack, Sylvia K., ed. **The Writer's Handbook**. Boston, Mas, 1989.

Carroll, David L. **How To Prepare Your Manuscript For A Publisher**. New York, NY, 1988.

Cassill, R.V. **Writing Fiction**. New York, NY, 1975.

Chilton Book Company. **Chilton's Repair Manual: Chevrolet/ GMC Pick-Ups and Suburban 1970-87**. Radnor, PA, 1988.

Collier, Oscar and Leighton, Frances Spatz. **How to Write and Sell Your First Novel**. Cincinnati, OH, 1986.

Curtis, Richard. **Beyond The Bestseller: A Literary Agent Takes You Inside The Book Business**. Markham, Ontario, 1989.

Daigh, Ralph. **Maybe You Should Write a Book**. New York, NY, 1977.

Delton, Judy. **The 29 Most Common Writing Mistakes and How To Avoid Them**. Cincinnati, OH, 1985.

Dibell, Ansen. **Plot**. Cincinnati, OH, 1988.

Frey, James N. **How To Write A Damn Good Novel**. New York, NY, 1987.
Gage, Cully. **The Northwoods Reader**. AuTrain, MI, 1987.

Gardner, John. **On Becoming A Novelist**. New York, NY, 1983.

Gee, Robin, ed. 1991 **Novel & Short Story Writer's Market**. Cincinnati, OH, 1990.

Goldberg, Natalie. **Writing Down the Bones**. Boston, MA, 1986.

Greene, James and Lewis, David. **Know Your Own Mind**. New York, NY, 1983.

Groom, Winston. **Forest Gump**. Garden City, NY, 1986.

Hall, Oakley. **The Art & Craft of Novel Writing**. Cincinnati, OH, 1989.

Harfield, Darvin P. **Interview**. Pokagon State park, IN, 1990.

Hensley, Dennis E. **Become Famous, Then Rich: How to Promote Yourself and Your Business**. Indianapolis, IN, 1983.

Hensley, Dennis E. and Miller, Holly G. **The Freelance Writer's Handbook**. New York, NY, 1987.

Helitzer, Melvin. **Comedy Writing Secrets**. Cincinnati, OH, 1987.

Herman, Jeff. **Insider's Guide To Book Editors, Publishers, And Literary Agents**. Rocklin, CA, 1992.

Hogins, James Burl and Yarber, Robert E. **Reading Writing And Rhetoric**. Chicago, IL, 1972.

Holt, Robert Lawrence. **How To Publish, Promote, And Sell Your Own Book**. New York, NY, 1985.

Howard, Kathleen and Gibat, Norman. **The Lore of Still Building**. Fostoria, OH, 1991.

Kellogg, J.H. **The Home Hand-Book Of Domestic Hygiene And Rational Medicine**. Battle Creek, MI, 1896.

Kent, Jean. **The Professional Writers' Phrase Book**. New York, NY, 1987.

Knott, Blanche. **Truly Tasteless Jokes**. New York, NY, 1982.

Kremer, John. **Book Marketing Made Easier**. Fairfield, IA, 1991.

Kremer, John. **1001 ways to market your book**. Fairfield, IA, 1993.

Larsen, Michael. **Literary Agents: How to Get & Work with the Right One for You**. Cincinnati, OH, 1986.

Leonard, George. **The Ice Cathedral**. New York, NY, 1984.

McCormick, Mona. **The Fiction Writer's Research Handbook**. New York, NY, 1988.

Meyer, Kathlene. **How To Shit In The Woods**. Berkely, CA, 1989.

Miller, Holly G. **How To Earn More Than Pennies For Your Thoughts**. Anderson, IN, 1990.

Monroe, Robert. **Journeys Out Of The Body**. Garden City, NY, 1977.

Neff, Glenda Tennant, ed. **1991 Writer's Market**. Cincinnati, OH, 1990.

Nolan, William F. **How To Write Horror Fiction**. Cincinnati, OH, 1990.

Nonymous, A. and Smilin, Uar. **What The Hell Is Going On Here?**. Sedona, AZ, 1999.

Parker, Roger C. **Looking Good In Print**. Chapel Hill, NC, 1990.

Perret, Gene. **Comedy Writing Workbook**. New York, NY, 1990.

Plimpton, George, ed. **The Writer's Chapbook**. New York, NY, 1989.

Polking, Kikr, ed. **Writer's Friendly Legal Guide**. Cincinnati, OH, 1989.

Poszar, Adam. **Interview**. Pokagon State Park, IN, 1990.

Poynter, Dan. **The Self-Publishing Manual**. Santa Barbara, CA, 1991.

Poynter, Dan. **Publishing Short Run Books**. Santa Barbara, CA, 1988.

Provost, Gary. **Make Every Word Count**. Cincinnati, OH, 1986.

Rico, Gabriele Lusser. **Writing the Natural Way**. Los Angeles, CA, 1983.

Roberts, Wess. **Leadership Secrets Of Atilla The Hun.** New York, NY, 1987.

Rule, Lareina. **Name Your Baby.** New York, NY, 1988.

Shipley, Joseph T. **Dictionary Of Word Origins.** New York, NY, 1945.

Songwriter Unknown. *Drop-Kick Me Jesus Through The Goalpost Of Life.* Place and year of pub'n unknown.

Staake, Bob,ed, and Shaughnessy, Roseann, ed. **1993 Humor And Cartoon Markets.** Cincinnati, OH, 1992.

Swain, Dwight V. **Creating Characters: How to Build Story People.** Cincinnati, OH, 1990.

Troyat, Henri. **Ivan The Terrible.** New York, NY, 1987.

Turco, Lewis. **Dialogue.** Cincinnati, OH, 1989.

Ueland, Brenda. **If You Want To Write.** Saint Paul, MN, 1987.

Unknown. *Your Space Or Mine?* Observed on front of tee shirt, Franklin Park Mall, Toledo, Ohio, October 21, 1983.

Unknown, assumed to be same as above. *If Today Is Thursday, This Must Be Earth, Right?* Observed on back of same tee shirt as above, same date.

Varga, Andrew. **Interviews.** February, April, June, August, October, December, 1990. Somewhere, IN.

Vonnegut, Kurt. **Hocus Pocus.** New York, NY, 1990.

Wallin, Craig. **Backyard Cash Crops.** Bellingham, WA, 1992.

Whitehouse, James. **Interviews.** January, March, May, July September, November, 1990. Somewhere, MI.

Zinsser, William. **Writing To Learn.** New York, NY, 1988.

INDEX

Topic

* Designates topics that were;
    a) edited out at the last minute,
    b) beyond the authors' levels of comprehension,
    c) added accidentally,
    d) misspelled intentionally,
    e) mentioned just for fun,
     or
    f) forgotten entirely.

AND NOW

(Finally)

How To Become A Rich And Famous Author Without Ever Really Writing A Book

In order to become a rich and famous author, you have to act in a manner that assumes you already ARE a rich and famous author. Yes, imitate. Its that easy. Here are some things that have made people stand out as successful authors, or at least will make you stand out as one.

1. Wear glasses. Anybody who is anybody in the writing trade wears them. The more unique (old-fashioned, taped at the hinges, day-glo yellow) the better.

2. Buy and carry a pipe. Not the plastic bubble kind or the ones made out of corn cobs. Buy a real pipe, carry it in one hand always (you can set it down when you take a shower), and smoke it in public. If you are unfortunate enough to be a confirmed non-smoker you can either leave the bowl empty and make occasional sucking sounds with it or, with a little practice, you can put a small amount of baby powder in the bowl and blow into the stem for effect as the mood strikes you. Don't do this if you are a woman. Hard as it is to believe, a woman who smokes a pipe is still a tad too weird even for writers. Buy those skinny little cigars instead. Again, if you don't REALLY smoke, there are candy and chewing gum look-alikes that can hardly be discerned from the genuine items.

3. Memorize the names of a dozen superstar authors and talk about them as if you are a personal friend -better yet, the only personal friend- of each one. Quote them often in conversation. Most impressive in today's literary circles are Russian authors. Preferably dead ones. In fact, it is much better to "know" and quote lots of dead authors. We would, however, caution against doing this with names such as Shakespeare, Hemingway, and Longfellow. It can be even more effective to publicly be close friends with authors no one else has ever heard of, so feel free to make them up if the mood strikes you. Please remember, if you are referring to a foreign author, always speak his or her name with an accent.

4. Next, memorize the names of six or seven publishing firms and casually mention from time to time that you spoke with so-and-so there just last week. So-and-so is, of course, the chief editor. Use any person's name you want. Editors change jobs so fast that nobody can keep track of them. Memorizing the names of the publishing companies is easier than you may think. You only have to remember their first names. Better still, their initials.

If, for example, you find a publisher called, Harley, Fox, Berkowitz, and MacGregor, you need only to remember either Harley or HFB&M. You could, in this example, sound additionally exclusive by referring to it simply as B&M.

If anyone should happen to ask about them in conversation, merely tilt your head as far back as you can and still be able to maintain eye contact and say, "I see that YOU don't know publishing."

5. Change your name. Some suggestions for good names to use today are Stephan Kang, Berry Sewart, Deter Strawb, Ian Mice, Bean Awuelle, James Clavicle, Robert Budrum, Jane Michelar, and Eddie Alton Powe. If spoken quickly and indistinctly enough, you will impress many people. And if you ever decide to really publish a book, those who skim book covers in search of their favorite authors will not notice a thing until after they have bought your book. This is known in the industry as "built in" sales, based on the Barnum or Sucker theory.

6. You must also purchase two suits.

The first suit must be white. All white. White jacket, white pants, white shirt, white tie, white socks, white shoes, white belt, white Panama hat, etc. The second suit must be identical to the first, except black. Wear them on alternate days. No deviations.

No, ladies, skirts or dresses are not recommended. Pants. You may add gloves if you wish, but only if they are either white or black and worn with the matching suits.

For those of you who choose to ignore us and wear skirts anyway, your hemlines MUST be at least three and one-half inches longer than current fashion dictates.

7. It would also be helpful if you were to locate a dictionary of seldom- or never-used words. Again, memorize a dozen or so and use them often. If memorization is not your forte, make some up, nobody will know the difference if they sound impressive enough. Here's a hint. Orgasms are big these days. Take an ordinary word and add -gasm to the end. Your favorite athletic team winning by a wide margin might be referred to as a sportsgasm. (Go easy, however, on discussing sports; they are for commoners, unlike your new self.) You may refer to Maserrati's latest vehicular blur as an autogasm. Your obvious writing and publishing success could be a blazegasm.

8. It is also helpful and impressive to use, and even create, acronyms. Readers have to pause to decipher them, thereby creating respect for your obviously superb ability with the language. GREAT

CARE must be taken regarding the relationship between the acronyms used and the persons or firms to whom you are writing. Here is an example of a common acronym.

SSAE: Now, to anyone who writes professionally or even those who send away for all that neat stuff listed in the back of most magazines, this represents a Stamped, Self-Addressed Envelope.

If you happen to be writing a letter to an American automaker, however, they might assume you were proposing a suggestion; Start Studying Auto Emissions. In a couple of months, you will probably receive a terse reply to the effect, "Thank you for your suggestion. Negative financial influx currently dictates personnel reorganization directly impacting your recommended endeavor indefinitely."

Should you happen to drop the acronym into a short note to a Japanese automaker, they will naturally assume that you are talking about a Self Starting Auto Engine. You will get an immediate response admitting that they have been working on it for the past five years and insisting to know how you found out about it.

Should these four letters fall into a request to a television news service, it will probably be read as See Story At Eleven. You will be inundated with phone calls asking for a copy of the video tape.

If you happen to drop a short note to your Auntie Emm and include this one, she may quite possibly read Safe Sex Avoids Embarrassment. You might find to your great discomfort that you are now her favorite niece or nephew.

Extreme care must also be taken when creating original acronyms. Here are a few examples of those to avoid.

Ten	Self	Car	Boys	First
Overly	Help	Racing	Airplane	Among
Amorous	Involves	And	Racing	Rotund
Dudes	Time	Prestige	Finals	Tenors

9. Send a friend to a bookstore in a far away metropolis. Have him ask for your novel (You'll need to have a name for it. See the chapter on Titles.), already a best seller -even before publication- hinting that he/she is surprised that a store of THEIR reputation would certainly carry it and hint that the paper stated that you are doing a book signing there on the next day. Have the friend also casually mention that your novel will be shipped (in humongous quantities) to arrive the day prior to your arrival, referring to the newspaper article, of course. If they get any static, have them mutter something using the words CORPORATE and ANGRY.

10. Go to the bookstore the next afternoon, in one of your suits of course. Bring a pen, folding chair, and card table. Set them up JUST OUTSIDE the door to the business. When an employee comes out to ask you what the hell you're doing, speak VERY LOUDLY about the books not having arrived on time and how your whole promo tour will be thrown awry schedule-wise. INSIST that the District Manager be notified immediately concerning the botched order. Repeat this in at least seven other bookstores as soon as you can.

11. If you insist on adding a sense of legitimacy to your greatness, you will probably want to involve a real publisher somewhere along the way. Here's how to do it. Find the names and addresses of twenty to twenty-four publishers. If you can get the names of their senior editors, so much the better. If you can't, use "Senior Editor".

Don't worry about which publishers, you can pick them at random from books such as 'Writer's Market', 'Literary Market Place', or the inside covers of any books that catch your eye on the shelves of your local library or drug store check-out line.

Send the following letter to each of them. You can either write the letter yourself or you can photocopy the one below, scratch out the instructions, and pencil in the right figures. They'll never notice.

Be sure to use a heavy, dark pencil with a soft lead.

Put your pseudonym here.
Put your address here.
(If you have a Post Office Box, use it. If you don't, get one.
Don't use your home address! It isn't businesslike.)
(This is called a letterhead.)

Put the Date here

Put the person's name or "Senior Editor" here.
Name of publisher
Address - the publisher's, not yours! City, State, Zip

Dear (Repeat person's name or use "Senior Editor" again.):

I am possessed by ambitions such that I cannot rest until I have at least (pick a number from three to seventeen) titles recorded simultaneously in the 'New York Times' Best Seller List.

I am sending this letter to you, and you only, because of the ideal, perfect, unique (Choose one.) match between your present catalog and my artistic voice resulting from my (pick a number from one to eight) years of research in the publishing industry.

All the works mentioned above are complete and ready to go to press.

Have your people contact mine and we'll do lunch. My office number is (Make up a number! DO NOT use your real phone number!)

I look forward to hearing from you soon.

Sincerely,

Sign your pseudonym (pen name - see the appropriate chapter) here.
NEVER use your real name.

12. Wait a week and send the following letter:

Repeat your letterhead here.

Put the date here.

Repeat the person's name here, or use "Senior Editor" again
Ditto the address.

Dear Sir:

     Please forgive my late reply to your letter of (Put the date of
your original letter here.) I have been forced to search for a new
literary agent as my old one just cannot keep up with the volume of
material I am currently producing.

     Furthermore, he was not satisfied with the latest $(pick a
number between 75,000 and 1.5 million) contract that I settled for
with (Pick the name of another publisher, or make one up). As my
search has not yet produced an agent to my liking, I am unfortunately
forced to negotiate my own contracts on a temporary basis.

     Enclosed is the outline and first chapter of my latest en-
deavor. Offer what you will and I'll get back to you.

Sincerely,

(Your pen name here)

     Whatever you do, send only the letter. Mail it in the biggest
envelope you can find. Do not include anything else. In just a few days
your Post Office box will be chock full of letters from publishers
begging to see your work.

     Reply to each one by sending the following telegram.

Can't stop. Stop.
Death in family. Stop.
Finances in trouble. Stop. Manuscripts will be
sent as soon as i can afford postage. Stop.
Advance? Stop. (Your pen name here.) Stop.

13. Now you have only to sit back, prop your feet up, and wait for the money to roll in. Not only will you become rich, but when word gets out- you'll be really famous, too! Now you can afford to buy that expensive home you've always dreamed of. Go ahead, just don't tell anybody where you've moved to.

14. Maybe this sounds like a lot of work to you. If so, you can possibly get an agent to do it for you, using letters similar to the ones suggested above. In your first letter to the agent, add the following statement.

> My level of literary ambition is such that, were it applied to the art of warfare, it would have fainted Tamerlane, the ancient warlord whose most memorable activity was to pile the heads of his fallen enemies, occasionally tens of thousands at a time, into pyramids at the entrances to the cities he had conquered.

The inclusion of the above statement will not only let your new agent know that you are gung-ho and mean business, it will also intimate that you have read some of those musty old history books.

Agents and editors like that.

HINT: You might not want to include this statement if you are trying to impress the publisher of children's books. Its up to you.

EPILOGUE

The only situation that we have not addressed is that of someone who genuinely wants to become a writer. You know the kind; they eat, sleep, and shine WRITER. To the few of you to whom this applies, we have three pieces of advice:

Don't use cliches.

DON'T QUIT

and

NEVER, EVER GIVE UP!

P.S. If all else fails, write a how to book.
P.P.S. We lied about almost everything.
 Have a nice Day.

We know how much you have enjoyed this book.*

We are including an order form on the last page so that you can purchase more copies as birthday, retirement, anniversary, Mothers' Day, Arbor Day, Secretaries Day, Groundhog Day, Fourth of July, Presidents Day, Grandparents Day, Sweetest Day, or Lief Eriksson Day gifts for your family, friends, acquaintances, or complete strangers.

In addition, if you really hated this book, buy copies for your enemies -and get them where it hurts!

* If, at this point, you are saying to yourself, "You gotta be kidding," all we can reply is that you read this far before you found out?!

This page has been left blank intentionally
for your convenience.

We tell you this because we strongly believe
that you, the reader,
deserve to be informed.

Nothing has been printed here.

This was done on purpose.

The authors and editors of this book,
after much discussion and negotiation,
decided that it would leave a much better impression
on you, the reader, if this page was left blank.

You know, for notes or whatever.

So we did just that,
left this page blank intentionally.

You won't find any marks on this page,
not even the page number.

You are being told this in order to avoid confusion within
your own mind.

By the way, none of this exists.

Thank you.

Order Form

Please send me _____ copies of The Fictional Writer's Primer.

Name: _____

Address: _____

City: _____ State: _____ Zip: _____

Price $6.95 per copy.

Sales Tax:
Please add 5% for books shipped to Hoosiers (Indiana residents).

Shipping:
$3.00 for first book. $1.00 for each additional.

Amount enclosed: _____

Please send check or money order in US funds to:

Rabid Rhino Publishing
PO Box 5013
Huntington, IN 46750

☐ Check here if you would like to receive word
of our upcoming zany works.

IT'S FREE *!*